ASPECTS
of PSYCHOLO

# PSYCHOPATHOLOGY

# PSYCHOPATHOLOGY

RICHARD GROSS & ROB MCILVEEN

Hodder & Stoughton

A MEMBER OF THE HODDER HEADLINE GROUP

# Dedication

To all students of Psychology: past, present and future

*British Library Cataloguing in Publication Data*
A catalogue record for this title is available from the British Library

ISBN  0 340 78032 0

First published  2000
Impression number    10  9  8  7  6  5  4  3  2  1
Year    2004   2003   2002   2001   2000

Typeset by GreenGate Publishing Services, Tonbridge, Kent.
Printed and bound in Great Britain for Hodder and Stoughton Educational, a division of
Hodder Headline plc, 338 Euston Road, London NW1 3BH,
by Cox & Wyman, Reading, Berks

# CONTENTS

# PREFACE

The *Aspects of Psychology* series aims to provide a short and concise, but detailed and highly accessible, account of selected areas of psychological theory and research.

*Psychopathology* consists of four chapters. Chapter 1 discusses the characteristics, types and explanations of schizophrenia, whilst Chapter 2 looks at the characteristics and explanations of depression. Chapter 3 deals with anxiety disorders, and in Chapter 4 we consider anorexia nervosa and bulimia disorder.

For the purposes of revision, we have included detailed summaries of the material presented in each chapter. Instead of a separate glossary, for easy reference the Index contains page numbers in **bold** which refer to definitions and main explanations of particular concepts.

# ACKNOWLEDGEMENTS

We would like to thank Dave Mackin, Anna Churchman and Denise Stewart at GreenGate Publishing for their swift and efficient preparation of the text. Thanks also to Greig Aitken at Hodder for all his hard work in coordinating this project, and to Tim Gregson-Williams for his usual help and support.

**Picture Credits**

The publishers would like to thank the following for permission to reproduce photographs and other illustrations in this book: p.4 (Fig 1.1), The Bridgeman Art Library, *The Garden of Earthly Delights: Hell*, right wing of triptych, detail of 'Tree Man', c1500 (panel), by Hieronymous Bosch (c1450–1516); p.49 (Fig 3.1), Science Photo Library; p.50 (Fig 3.2), Life File © Mike Maidment; p.61 (Fig 3.3), Rex Features, London © SIPA-PRESS; p.71 (Fig 4.1), Rex Features, London, Robin Palmer; p.73 (Fig 4.2) (left) Rex Features, London; (right) Yes! Magazine / Richard Barnes.

Every effort has been made to obtain necessary permission with reference to copyright material. The publishers apologise if inadvertently any sources remain unacknowledged and will be glad to make the necessary arrangements at the earliest opportunity.

# SCHIZOPHRENIA

## Introduction and overview

Of all the disorders identified in the tenth revision of the *International Standard Classification of Diseases, Injuries and Causes of Death: Mental and Behavioural Disorders* (ICD-10), and the fourth edition of the *Diagnostic and Statistical Manual of Mental Disorders* (DSM-IV), schizophrenia is the most serious. Kraepelin (1913) called the disorder dementia praecox (senility of youth), believing that it occurred early in adult life and was characterised by a progressive deterioration or dementia. However, Bleuler (1911) observed that it often began in later life and was not always characterised by dementia. Bleuler coined the word *schizophrenia* to refer to a *splitting* of the mind's various functions in which the personality loses its unity.

This chapter examines schizophrenia's nature, its characteristics and sub-types, and its course. Perhaps because of its nature, schizophrenia's causes have received more attention than any other mental disorder and many theories have been advanced to explain it. This chapter also examines the plausibility of these theories.

## The characteristics of schizophrenia

As noted, schizophrenia is a disorder in which personality loses its unity. It should not be confused with *multiple personality disorder*, in which personality splits into two or more separate *identities*. The confusion probably arises because the word *schizophrenia* derives from the Greek words *schizein* (to split) and *phren* (the mind). As will be seen, schizophrenia is a 'splitting' between thoughts and feelings, the consequences being bizarre and maladaptive behaviour.

In Britain, schizophrenia's diagnosis relies on *first-rank symptoms* (Schneider, 1959). The presence of one or more of these, in the absence of brain disease, is likely to result in a diagnosis of schizophrenia. The three first rank symptoms are *passivity experiences* and *thought disturbances, hallucinations,* and *primary delusions.*

## Passivity experiences and thought disturbances

These include *thought insertion* (the belief that thoughts are being inserted into the mind from outside, under the control of external forces), *thought withdrawal* (the belief that thoughts are being removed from the mind under the control of external forces), and *thought broadcasting* (the belief that thoughts are being broadcast or otherwise made known to others). External forces may include 'the Martians', 'the Communists' and 'the Government', and the mechanism by which thoughts are affected is often a 'special ray' or a radio transmitter. Thought broadcasting is also an example of a *delusion* (see below).

## Hallucinations

Hallucinations are perceptions of stimuli not actually present. They may occur in any sense modality, but the most common are *auditory*. Typically, voices come from outside the individual's head and offer a 'running commentary' on behaviour in the third person (such as 'He is washing his hands. Now he'll go and dry them.'). Often, they will comment on the individual's character, usually insultingly, or give commands.

*Somatosensory* hallucinations involve changes in how the body feels. It may, for example, be described as 'burning' or 'numb'. *Depersonalisation*, in which the person reports feeling separated from the body, may also occur. Hallucinations are often distortions of real environmental perceptual cues, so that noises from (say) a heating system are heard as voices whispering (Frude, 1998).

**Box 1.1** *What causes auditory hallucinations?*

Bick & Kinsbourne (1987) propose that at least some auditory hallucinations may be projections of the individual's own thoughts. Friston (cited in Highfield, 1995) has shown that there is a breakdown in 'dialogue' between the frontal lobes (which deal with intentions) and the temporal lobes (which process language and register the consequences of actions). This results in a failure to integrate behaviour with the perception of its consequences. In auditory hallucinations, normal thoughts may progress via internal language into a form in which they can be articulated and, if desired, spoken. This involves a feedback loop which warns the next stage of the process what is happening, and tells us that the inner speech is our own. Auditory hallucinations may occur because the feedback loop is broken. According to Friston, schizophrenics talk to themselves without realising it.

## Primary delusions

Delusions are false beliefs which persist even in the presence of disconfirming evidence. A delusion of grandeur is the belief that one is somebody who is or was important or powerful (such as Jesus Christ or Napoleon). A delusion of persecution is the belief that one is being plotted or conspired against, or being interfered with by certain people or organised groups. A *delusion of reference* is the belief that objects, events and so on have a (typically negative) personal significance. For example, a person may believe that the words of a song specifically refer to him or her. A *delusion of nihilism* is the belief that nothing really exists and that all things are simply shadows. The belief that one has been dead for years and is observing the world from afar is also common. All delusions are held with extraordinary conviction, and the deluded individual may be so convinced of their truth that they are acted on, even if this involves murder.

**Box 1.2** *Capgras syndrome*

Sufferers of Capgras syndrome believe that family members and others are *imposters*. Ramachandran & Hirstein (cited in Johnston,1997) report the case of D.S., who suffered damage to the right side of his brain following a traffic accident. D.S. shows no physiological response to people's faces or pictures of himself, and is convinced that his parents are 'doubles'. Ramachandran and Hirstein believe that when we meet people, the brain creates memory 'files' about them. When we next meet them, our emotional responses cause their files to be retrieved rather than new ones opened. This does not happen in Capgras syndrome because the links between pattern recognition and emotion have been severed.

**Figure 1.1** *There is considerable similarity between the paintings produced by psychotic patients and this section of a picture of Hell, painted by the sixteenth-century Dutch painter Hieronymus Bosch*

First rank symptoms are subjective experiences and can only be inferred on the basis of the individual's verbal reports. According to Slater & Roth (1969), hallucinations are the least important first rank symptom because they are not exclusive to schizophrenia (which is also true of delusions: see Chapter 2). Slater and Roth identify four different characteristics of schizophrenia directly observable from behaviour. These are *thought process disorder, disturbances of affect, psychomotor disorders* and *lack of volition.*

## Thought process disorder

Although constantly bombarded by sensory information, we are usually able to selectively attend to some and exclude the rest. This ability is impaired in schizophrenia and leads to overwhelming and unintegrated ideas and sensations, which affect concentration. Thus, schizophrenics are easily distracted. Their failure to maintain an attentional focus is reflected in the inability to maintain a focus of thought. In turn, this is reflected in the inability to maintain a focus in language.

The classic disturbance in the *form* of schizophrenic thought (as opposed to its *content*) involves *loose associations*. In these, the individual shifts from topic to topic as new associations arise, and fails to form coherent and logical thoughts. As a result, language is often rambling and disjointed. Often, one idea triggers an association with another. When associations become too loose, incoherence results (a *word salad*).

---

**Box 1.3**   *Loose associations and word salad*

I am the nun. If that's enough, you are still his. That is a brave cavalier, take him as your husband, Karoline, you well know, though you are my Lord, you were just a dream. If you are the dove-cote, Mrs K. is still beset by fear. Otherwise I am not so exact in eating. Handle the gravy carefully. Where is the paint brush? Where are you, Herman? (From Bleuler, 1911)

---

A word's sound may also trigger an association with a similar sounding word (*clang association*) as in:

**'The King of Spain feels no pain in the drain of the crane. I'm lame, you're tame: with fame, I'll be the same'.**

Schizophrenic thought is also reflected in *neologisms*, the invention of new words (such as *glump* and *wooger*), or the combination of existing words in a unique fashion (such as 'belly bad luck and brutal and outrageous' to describe stomach ache). Other characteristics include *thought blocking, literal interpretation* and *poverty of content*.

## Disturbances of affect

In some cases, thought process disorder may be brief and intermittent. However, disturbances of affect (or *emotional disturbances*), and other characteristic disturbances tend to be fairly stable. The three main types of emotional disturbance are *blunting, flattened affect* and *inappropriate affect*.

### Blunting

This is an apparent lack of emotional sensitivity, in which the individual remains impassive in response to events that would ordinarily evoke a strong emotional reaction. For example, when told that a close relative had died, a schizophrenic might respond in a monotonic voice: 'Really? Is that so?'

### Flattened affect

This is a more pervasive and general absence of emotional expression in which the person appears devoid of any sort of emotional tone. Flattened affect may reflect the schizophrenic's 'turning off' for self-protection from stimuli s/he is incapable of dealing with (Mednick, 1958).

### Inappropriate affect

This is the display of an emotion which is incongruous with its context. For example, when asked if a meal was enjoyable or when offered a gift, a schizophrenic may become agitated and violent. However, the receipt of bad news may be followed by uncontrolled giggling.

## Psychomotor disorders

In some schizophrenics, motor behaviour is affected. In catatonia, the individual assumes an unusual posture which is maintained for hours or even days. Attempts to alter the posture are usually met with resistance and sometimes violence. In *stereotypy*, the person engages in purposeless, repetitive movements, such as rocking back and forth or knitting an imaginary sweater. Instead of being mute and unmoving, the individual may be wild and excited, showing frenetically high levels of motor activity.

## Lack of volition

This is the tendency to withdraw from interactions with other people. It sometimes involves living an asocial and secluded life, through loss of drive, interest in the environment, and so on. More disturbed individuals appear to be oblivious to others' presence and completely unresponsive when people like friends and relatives attempt contact.

# Types of schizophrenia

Both ICD-10 and DSM-IV distinguish between different types of schizophrenia. This is because the disorder's characteristics are so variable.

## Hebephrenic schizophrenia

The most severe type of schizophrenia is *hebephrenic* (or *disorganised*) *schizophrenia* (hebephrenic means 'silly mind'). It is most often diagnosed in adolescence and young adulthood, and is usually progressive and irreversible. Its main characteristics are incoherence of language, disorganised behaviour, disorganised delusions, vivid hallucinations (often sexual or religious) and a loosening of associations. It is also characterised by flattened or inappropriate affect and by extreme social withdrawal and impairment.

## Simple schizophrenia

This usually appears during late adolescence and has a slow, gradual onset. Principally, the individual withdraws from reality, has difficulty in making or maintaining friends, is aimless and lacks drive, and shows a decline in academic or occupational performance. Males often become drifters or tramps, whilst females may become prostitutes. Simple schizophrenia is only recognised by ICD-10 which, whilst acknowledging that it is controversial, retains it because some countries still use it.

## Catatonic schizophrenia

The major characteristic of catatonic schizophrenia is a striking impairment of motor activity. Individuals may hold unusual and difficult positions until their limbs grow swollen, stiff and blue from lack of movement. A particularly striking feature is *waxy flexibility*, in which the individual maintains a position into which he or she has been manipulated by others.

Catatonic schizophrenics may engage in *agitated catatonia*, bouts of wild, excited movement, and may become dangerous and unpredictable. In *mutism*, the person is apparently totally unresponsive to external stimuli. However, catatonic schizophrenics often *are* aware of what others were saying or doing during the catatonic episode, as evidenced by their reports after the episode has subsided. Another characteristic is *negativism*, in which the individual sits either motionless and resistant to instructions or does the opposite of what has been requested.

## Paranoid schizophrenia

This has the presence of well-organised, delusional thoughts as its dominant characteristic. Paranoid schizophrenics show the highest level of awareness and least impairment in the ability to carry out daily functions. Thus, language and behaviour appear relatively normal. However, the delusions are usually accompanied by hallucinations which are typically consistent with them. It tends to have a later onset than the other schizophrenias, and is the most homogenous type (paranoid schizophrenics are more alike than simple, catatonic and hebephrenic schizophrenics).

## Undifferentiated (or atypical) schizophrenia

This is a 'catch-all' category for people who either fit the criteria for more than one type, or do not appear to be of any clear type. For example, disorders of thought, perception and emotion, without the features particular to the types described above, would result in the label undifferentiated being applied.

## Other disorders

These include *schizophreniform psychosis* (similar to schizophrenia, but lasting for less than 6 months), *schizotypal disorder* (eccentric behaviour and unusual thoughts and emotions resembling those of schizophrenia, but without characteristic schizophrenic abnormalities), and *schizoaffective disorder* (episodes in which both schizophrenic and affective characteristics are prominent, but which do not justify a diagnosis of either schizophrenia or an affective disorder).

# The course of schizophrenia

The characteristics of schizophrenia rarely appear in 'full-blown' form. Typically, there are three phases in schizophrenia's development. The *prodromal phase* usually occurs in early adolescence (*process schizophrenia*), or in relatively well-adjusted people in early adulthood (*reactive schizophrenia*). The individual becomes less interested in work, school, leisure activities and so on. Typically, he/she becomes increasingly withdrawn, eccentric, emotionally flat, cares little for health and appearance, and shows lowered productivity at either work or school. This phase may last from a few weeks to years.

In the second or *active phase*, the major characteristics of schizophrenia appear. This phase varies in its duration. In some people, it lasts only a few months, whereas in others it lasts a lifetime. If and when this phase subsides (usually when therapy is given), the person enters the *residual phase*. This is characterised by a lessening of the major characteristics and a more-or-less return to the prodromal phase. Around 25 per cent of schizophrenics regain the capacity to function normally, ten per cent remain permanently in the active phase and 50–65 per cent alternate between the residual and active phases (Bleuler, 1978).

---

**Box 1.4** *The concept of schizophrenia*

Whether schizophrenia is a single disorder with several types, or whether each type is a distinct disorder has been hotly debated. Gelder *et al.* (1989) believe that, with the possible exception of paranoid schizophrenia, the other types are actually of doubtful validity and difficult to distinguish between in clinical practice. Because of this lack of reliability, it has been argued that the concept of schizophrenia is 'almost hopelessly in tatters' and that there is no such entity as schizophrenia (Carson, 1989; Sarbin, 1992).

---

# Explanations of schizophrenia

## Behavioural model

According to the behavioural model, schizophrenia can be explained in terms of conditioning and observational learning. Ullman & Krasner (1969) argue that people show schizophrenic behaviour when it is more likely than normal behaviour to be reinforced. In psychiatric institutions, staff may unintentionally reinforce schizophrenic behaviour by paying more attention to those displaying it. Patients can 'acquire' the characteristics by observing others being reinforced for behaving bizarrely. Alternatively, schizophrenia may be acquired through the *absence* of reinforcement for attending to appropriate objects.

Certainly, schizophrenic behaviour can be modified through conditioning, although little evidence suggests that such techniques can affect the expression of thought disorders. Moreover, it is difficult to see how schizophrenic behaviour patterns can be *acquired* when people have had no opportunity to observe them. For these reasons at least, it is generally accepted that the behavioural model contributes little to understanding schizophrenia's *causes* (Frude, 1998).

## Psychodynamic model

One psychodynamic explanation proposes that schizophrenia results from an ego which has difficulty in distinguishing between the self and the external world. Another account attributes it to a *regression* to an infantile stage of functioning. Freud believed that schizophrenia occurred when a person's ego either became overwhelmed by the demands of the id, or was besieged by unbearable guilt from the superego (see Gross & McIlveen, 1998).

Rather than resolving the intense *intrapsychic conflict*, the ego retreats to the oral stage of psychosexual development, where the infant has not yet learned that it and the world are separate. Initially, *regressive symptoms* occur, and the individual may experience delusions of self-importance. Fantasies become confused with reality, which gives rise to hallucinations and delusions (Freud called these *restitutional symptoms*), as the ego attempts to regain reality.

The incoherent delusions and bizarre speech patterns displayed in schizophrenia *may* make sense when preceded by the phrase 'I dreamed ...'. However, the fact that schizophrenic behaviour is not that similar to infantile behaviour, and the psychodynamic model's inability to predict schizophrenic outcome on the basis of theoretically predisposing early experiences, has resulted in it being given little credibility.

## The role of social and family relationships

According to Bateson *et al.* (1956), parents predispose children to schizophrenia by communicating in ways that place them in 'no-win' situations. A father might, for example, complain about his daughter's lack of affection, whilst simultaneously telling her that she is too old to hug him when she tries to be affectionate. Bateson *et al.* used the term *double bind* to describe such contradictory multiple verbal and non-verbal messages. Children who experience double binds may lose their grip on reality and see their own feelings, perceptions, knowledge and so on as being unreliable indicators of it.

Similarly, *deviant communication* within families may lead to children doubting their own feelings and perceptions. Wynne *et al.* (1977) propose that some parents often refuse to recognise the meaning of words used by their children and instead substitute words of their own. This can be confusing if the children are young, and may play a role in schizophrenia's development.

---

**Box 1.5**  *Marital schism and mental skew*

Schizophrenics' families are frequently marked by *marital schism* or *marital skew* (Lidz, 1973). When both parents are preoccupied with their own problems, they threaten the household's continuity, and marital schism occurs. Marital skew occurs when one disturbed parent dominates the household. According to Fromm-Reichman (1948), the *schizophrenogenic* mother is one who generates schizophrenic children. Such mothers are seen as being domineering, cold, rejecting and guilt-producing. Fromm-Reichman argued that, in conjunction with a passive and ineffectual father, such mothers 'drive' their children to schizophrenia.

---

The view that social and family interactions play a causal role in schizophrenia's development lacks empirical support, and has difficulty in explaining why abnormal patterns develop in some rather than all the children in a family. Klebanoff (1959) has suggested that the family patterns correlated with schizophrenia actually constitute a *reasonable* response to an unusual child. Thus, children who were brain-damaged and retarded tended to have mothers that were more possessive and controlling than mothers of non-disturbed children. Although family factors probably do not play a causal role in the development of schizophrenia, how the family reacts to offspring when the symptoms have appeared may play a role in influencing an individual's functioning. In support of this, Doane *et al.* (1985) found that the recurrence of schizophrenic symptoms was reduced when parents reduced their hostility, criticism and intrusiveness towards the offspring.

## Cognitive model

As noted previously, schizophrenia is characterised by disturbances in thought, perception, attention and language. The cognitive model views these as *causes* rather than *consequences* of the disorder. Maher (1968) sees the bizarre use of language as a result of faulty information processing. When words with multiple meanings to an individual (*vulnerable words*) are used, a person may respond in a personally relevant but semantically irrelevant or inappropriate way.

The cognitive model proposes that catatonic schizophrenia may be the result of a breakdown in *auditory selective attention*. Because our information processing abilities are limited, we need to purposefully select information to process. Impairment of the selective attention mechanism would result in the senses being bombarded with information. The catatonic schizophrenic's lack of interaction with the outside world may occur because it is the only way in which sensory stimulation can be kept to a manageable level (Pickering, 1981: see Box 1.7).

## Medical model

### Genetic influences

Schizophrenia has a tendency to run in families. The likelihood of a person developing it is about one in 100. However, with one schizophrenic parent, the likelihood increases to one in five. If both parents are schizophrenic, it increases to about one in two or one in three. These observations have led some researchers to propose that schizophrenia can be explained in *genetic* terms.

---

**Box 1.6**   *Concordance and discordance*

One method of studying the inheritance of characteristics involves comparing the *resemblance* of identical and non-identical twins (and, in very rare cases, quadruplets: see Rosenthal, 1963). With *continuous* characteristics (e.g. intelligence test scores), resemblance is defined in terms of *correlation*. However, schizophrenia is considered to be *discontinuous* (a person either is schizophrenic or is not) and resemblance is defined in terms of a *concordance* rate. If two twins are schizophrenic, they are *concordant* for schizophrenia. If one is schizophrenic and the other is not, they are *discordant*.

---

Gottesman & Shields (1972) looked at the history of 45,000 individuals treated at two London hospitals between 1948 and 1964. They identified 57 schizophrenics with twins, who agreed to participate in their study. Using diagnosis and hospitalisation as the criteria for schizophrenia, the researchers reported a concordance rate of 42 per cent for identical (monozygotic or MZ) twins and nine per cent for non-identical (dizygotic or DZ) twins.

Other studies have consistently reported concordance rates which are higher for MZs than DZs (see Table 1.1, page 15). In *all* of them, though, the concordance rate is less than the theoretically expected 100 per cent. However, Heston (1970) found that if a MZ had a schizophrenic disorder, there was a 90 per cent chance that the other twin had *some sort* of mental disorder.

Of course, the *environment* may play an influential role, and given that twins tend to be raised in the same environment, it would be reckless to attribute Heston's (and others') findings exclusively to genetic factors. However, when MZs are separated at birth (and presumably raised in different environments), the concordance rate is as high as that obtained for MZs raised in the same environment (Gottesman, 1991).

Table 1.1   Concordance rates for schizophrenia for identical (MZ) and non-identical (DZ) twins (Based on Rose *et al.*, 1984)

| Study | 'Narrow' concordance * | | 'Broad' concordance * | |
|---|---|---|---|---|
| | % MZs | % DZs | % MZs | % DZs |
| Rosanoff *et al.* (1934) USA (41 MZs, 53 DZs) | 44 | 9 | 61 | 13 |
| Kallmann (1946) USA (174 MZs, 296 DZs) | 59 | 11 | 69 | 11–14 |
| Slater (1953) England (37 MZs, 58 DZs) | 65 | 14 | 65 | 14 |
| Gottesman & Shields (1966) England (24 MZs, 33 DZs) | 42 | 15 | 54 | 18 |
| Kringlen (1968) Norway (55 MZs, 90 DZs) | 25 | 7 | 38 | 10 |
| Allen *et al.* (1972) USA (95 MZs, 125 DZs) | 14 | 4 | 27 | 5 |
| Fischer (1973) Denmark (21 MZs, 41 DZs) | 24 | 10 | 48 | 20 |

(* 'Narrow' based on attempt to apply a relatively strict set of criteria when diagnosing schizophrenia. 'Broad' includes 'borderline schizophrenia', 'schizoaffective psychosis' and 'paranoid with schizophrenia-like features'.)

Clearly, looking at MZs reared apart is one way round the problem of controlling environmental factors. Another is to study children of schizophrenic parents brought up in foster or adoptive homes. The usual method is to compare the incidence of schizophrenia in the biological and adoptive parents of adopted children with the disorder. Heston (1966) compared 47 children of schizophrenic mothers adopted before the age of one month, with 50 children raised in the home of their biological and non-schizophrenic mothers. Psychiatrists' 'blind' testing of the children revealed that ten per cent with schizophrenic mothers were diagnosed as schizophrenic, whereas no children of non-schizophrenic mothers were so diagnosed. Also, children of schizophrenic mothers were more likely than children of non-schizophrenic mothers to be:

**'morally defective, sociopathic, neurotic, criminal and to have been discharged from the armed forces on psychiatric grounds' (Heston, 1966).**

Kety *et al.* (1968) examined Denmark's *Folkregister*, a lifelong record of Danish citizens. The researchers compiled lists of adopted children who either developed or did not develop schizophrenia. Its incidence in the adoptive families of those who developed the disorder (five per cent) was as low as in the adoptive families of those who did not develop it. However, in those who did develop schizophrenia its incidence in the biological families was far higher than expected (21 per cent). If the disposition towards schizophrenia is environmental, the incidence would be higher among adoptive relatives with whom the adopted child shared an environment. However, if hereditary factors are important, the incidence would be higher in biological than in adoptive relatives (which is what the researchers found). Klaning *et al.* (1996) have looked at the incidence of schizophrenia in twins *as a population* and found that it is higher than in the general population. This might be due to twins' greater exposure to perinatal complications (such as low birth weight), which could lower the 'threshold' for developing schizophrenia. Alternatively, the psychological environment might be different for twins and provide a greater risk of developing the disorder.

From what has been said, genetic factors appear to play some (and perhaps a major) role in schizophrenia. However, attempts to identify the gene or genes *responsible* have not been successful. Claims have been made about genetic markers on chromosomes 5 and 22, and then quickly retracted in the light of subsequent research. As noted, even if genes are involved, genetic factors alone cannot be responsible.

---

**Box 1.7**   *Chromosome 15 and the alpha-7 nicotinic receptor*

Many schizophrenics are chain smokers. This may not be coincidental. Research indicates that a genetic defect on chromosome 15 is responsible for a site in the brain (the alpha-7 nicotinic receptor) that plays a role in filtering information and which can be stimulated by nicotine (Freedman *et al.*, cited in Highfield, 1997a). This is the first time that malfunctioning neurons have been implicated in schizophrenia, and chain-smoking may be an unwitting form of 'self-medication'.

---

## Biochemical influences

One way in which genes may influence behaviour is through biochemical agents in the brain. According to the *inborn-error of metabolism hypothesis*, some people inherit a metabolic error which causes the body to break down naturally occurring chemicals into toxic ones which are responsible for schizophrenia's characteristics. Osmond & Smythies (1953) noted that there were similarities between the experiences of people who had taken hallucinogenic drugs and those of people diagnosed as schizophrenic. Some evidence supports the view that the brain produces its own *internal hallucinogens*. For example, Smythies (1976) found small amounts of hallucinogen-like chemicals in schizophrenics' cerebrospinal fluid, whilst Murray *et al.* (1979) reported that the hallucinogen *dimethyltryptamine* (DMT) was present in schizophrenics' urine. Moreover, when DMT levels decreased, schizophrenic symptoms also decreased. However, later research indicated that the characteristics of schizophrenia were *different* from those produced by hallucinogenic drugs, and researchers turned to other biochemicals.

Perhaps because hallucinogenic drugs are chemically similar to noradrenaline and dopamine (which occur naturally in the brain), these neurotransmitters became the focus of research, with dopamine receiving most attention. The earliest theory implicating dopamine proposed that schizophrenia was caused by its excess production, and post-mortem studies of diagnosed schizophrenics showed higher than normal concentrations of dopamine, especially in the limbic system (Iversen, 1979). However, rather than producing more dopamine *per se*, it is widely accepted that more dopamine is *utilised* as a result of overly sensitive post-synaptic receptors for it, or because of above normal reactivity to dopamine due to an increased number of receptor sites. For example, the density of one site (the D4 receptor) is six times greater in schizophrenic than non-schizophrenic brain tissue (Davis *et al.*, 1991).

Dopamine's role is supported by several lines of evidence. For example, in non-schizophrenics, cocaine and amphetamine produce delusions of persecution and hallucinations similar to those observed in some types of schizophrenia. Both drugs are known to cause the stimulation of dopamine receptors. Additionally, cocaine and amphetamine *exacerbate* schizophrenic symptoms (Davis, 1974). Research also indicates that drugs which treat schizophrenia reduce the concentration of brain-dopamine by blocking dopamine receptors and preventing them from becoming stimulated (Kimble, 1988).

**Box 1.8** *The diathesis–stress and vulnerability–stress models*

Genetic factors might create a predisposition towards schizophrenia which interacts with other factors to produce the disorder. Whilst most environments are conducive to normal development, some may trigger disorders like schizophrenia. The *diathesis–stress model* is one explanation of an interaction between genetic and biochemical factors, which accounts for the finding that not everybody who might be genetically predisposed to schizophrenia (by virtue of, say, having a schizophrenic parent) develops it.

The model proposes that schizophrenia occurs as a result of a biological vulnerability (*diathesis*) to a disorder interacting with personally significant environmental stressors. Genetic vulnerability puts a person at risk, but environmental stressors (like leaving home or losing a job) must be present for the gene to be 'switched on'. The *vulnerability–stress model* (Nuechterlein & Dawson, 1984) is an extension of the diathesis–stress model and specifies the genetically determined traits that can make a person vulnerable. These include hyperactivity and information-processing deficits.

Although the evidence linking dopamine to schizophrenia is impressive, its causal role has been questioned. For example, dopamine's availability could be just *one* factor in the sequence of schizophrenia's development rather than the only factor. More importantly, drugs used to treat schizophrenia are not always effective.

Drugs are evidently only helpful in treating what Kraepelin called the *positive* (or *Type 1*) *symptoms* of schizophrenia (Crow et al., 1982). These include the classic symptoms of delusions, hallucinations and thought disorder. The *negative* (or *Type 2*) *symptoms* of decreased speech, lack of drive, diminished social interaction and loss of emotional response, are little affected by drug treatment. This has led to the proposal that the positive symptoms have one cause (possibly related to dopamine), whereas the negative symptoms have some other cause.

## Neurodevelopmental influences

One possible cause of the negative symptoms is *brain damage*. There is evidence of structural abnormalities in schizophrenics' brains, which is 'powerful evidence that schizophrenia is a brain disease' (Johnson, 1989). Stevens (1982) showed that many schizophrenics display symptoms clearly indicating neurological disease, especially with regard to eye movements. These included decreased rate of eye blink, staring, lack of blink reflex in response to a tap on the forehead, poor visual pursuit movements, and poor pupillary reactions to light. Post-mortems suggested a disease that had occurred earlier in life and had partially healed, or one that was slowly progressing at the time of death.

Some schizophrenics underwent difficult births and their brains might have suffered a lack of oxygen (Harrison, 1995). The apparent decline in the number of cases of schizophrenia might be related to improvements in maternity care. Research using imaging devices to compare schizophrenic and non-schizophrenic brains has been reviewed by Chua & McKenna (1995). Several kinds of structural abnormality have been discovered in the schizophrenic brain, including an unusually small corpus collosum, high densities of white matter in the right frontal and parietal lobes, a smaller volume of temporal lobe grey matter, and unusually large ventricles (the hollow spaces in the brain filled with cerebrospinal fluid), indicating the loss of brain tissue elsewhere. However, Chua and McKenna argue that the only well-established structural abnormality in schizophrenia is lateral ventricular enlargement, and even this is modest and shows considerable overlap with the non-schizophrenic population. Whilst schizophrenia is not characterised by any simple focal reduction in brain activity, Chua and McKenna believe that complex alterations in the normal reciprocal patterns of activation between anatomically related areas of the cerebral cortex might characterise the disorder.

**Box 1.9** *The viral theory of schizophrenia*

If schizophrenia is the result of the brain's failure to develop normally for some reason (which would make it a *neurodevelopmental disorder*), it is important to know when this damage occurs. One theory suggests that the damage may be due to a *viral infection*. Seasonal variations in chickenpox and measles (both caused by viruses) are well known. The finding that significantly more people who develop schizophrenia are born in late winter and early spring than at other times of the year is not a statistical quirk (Torrey *et al.*, 1977).

Torrey (1988) believes that schizophrenia may be the result of a virus affecting pre-natal development, especially during the second trimester of pregnancy, when the developing brain is forming crucial interconnections. For example, in normal development, *pre-alpha cells* are formed in the middle of the brain and migrate towards the cortex. In schizophrenic brains, however, the cells get only 85 per cent of the way to their final destination. Support for a viral theory comes from longitudinal studies conducted by Barr *et al.* (1990) and O'Callaghan *et al.* (1991, 1993), who reported an increased risk for schizophrenia for those in the fifth month of foetal development during the 1957 *influenza pandemic*.

Bracha *et al.* (1991) have shown that one MZ twin who develops schizophrenia is significantly more likely to have various hand deformities compared with the other twin. Since the hands are formed during the second trimester of pregnancy, the same pre-natal trauma or virus which affects the brain may also affect the hands. To explain schizophrenia's tendency to run in families, Stevens (1982) has proposed that whatever causes the damage affects only people with an *inherited susceptibility* to schizophrenia and does not affect those with non-schizophrenic heredity.

At present, there is little agreement over the plausibility of viral theories. Some researchers, for example, have failed to find an association between births during the 1957 influenza epidemic and the later development of schizophrenia. It is ridiculous to suggest that the alleged schizophrenogenic effects of the epidemic were genuine and present in Finland, England, Wales and Edinburgh (as some studies have reported) but absent in the rest of Scotland and the United States (which other studies have found), since the virus that caused the epidemic could not have changed (Crow & Done, 1992).

Others have failed to find evidence of *any* significant associations between later schizophrenia and maternal exposure to a variety of infectious diseases other than influenza (O'Callaghan *et al.*, 1994). As Claridge (1987) has remarked, the season of birth effect has many equally plausible explanations, one being that it might reflect the cycles of sexual activity among the parents of future psychotics, a hypothesis which does not seem to have attracted much attention, despite its credibility as an explanation for the data.

What is likely, though, is that schizophrenia is *not* a result of a virus caught from domestic cats, a theory based on the observation that there is a higher incidence of the disorder in countries where cats are kept as pets (Bentall, 1996).

## Conclusions

This chapter has looked at schizophrenia's characteristics and various explanations for the disorder. Some are more plausible than others and have received considerable support. However, an explanation which is accepted by all of those working in the area so far remains elusive.

## Summary

- Schizophrenia is the most serious of all the disorders identified in ICD-10 and DSM-IV. In Britain, its diagnosis is based on Schneider's **first rank symptoms** (**passivity experiences** and **thought disorder**, **hallucinations**, and **primary delusions**).
- First rank symptoms can only be inferred from the individual's verbal reports. Four characteristics directly observable

from behaviour are **thought process disorder, disturbances of affect/emotional disturbances, psychomotor disturbances** and **lack of volition**.

- Both ICD-10 and DSM-IV distinguish between different types of schizophrenia. **Hebephrenic (disorganised), catatonic, paranoid**, and **undifferentiated** (or **atypical**) schizophrenias are recognised by both systems. ICD-10 also recognises **simple** schizophrenia.

- The course of schizophrenia is characterised by **prodromal, active,** and **residual phases**. The term **process schizophrenia** is used when the prodromal phase occurs in early adolescence. **Reactive schizophrenia** refers to the prodromal phase occurring in early adulthood. Around 25 per cent of schizophrenics regain the capacity to function normally, and ten per cent remain permanently in the active phase. Fifty to sixty-five per cent alternate between the residual and active phases.

- The **behavioural model** can account for schizophrenia's maintenance, but has difficulty explaining its origins. The **psychodynamic model**'s explanation is a poor predictor of a schizophrenic outcome. Neither model contributes much to understanding schizophrenia's causes.

- Social and family relationships (**double bind, deviant communication**, and **marital schism/skew**) have also been implicated in schizophrenia. However, it is difficult to explain why only **some** children in a family develop schizophrenia, and family patterns may be a response to an unusual child rather than a cause of abnormality.

- The observation that schizophrenia tends to run in families, and that schizophrenic parents have a greater chance of producing schizophrenic offspring, suggests that genetic factors may be involved in the disorder.

- There are higher **concordance rates** for schizophrenia in MZ than DZ twins, and a higher incidence of schizophrenia in **adopted** children of schizophrenic parents. Whilst genetic factors appear to play at least some role in schizophrenia, attempts to identify the gene or genes responsible have been equivocal.

- One way in which genes can influence behaviour is by altering **brain biochemistry**. The **inborn-error of metabolism** hypothesis claims that some people inherit a metabolic error. This causes their bodies to break down naturally occurring chemicals into toxic ones, which produce schizophrenia's symptoms.

- Another hypothesis proposes that the brain produces its own 'internal hallucinogens'. However, whilst early research found similarities between the effects of hallucinogenic drugs and the experiences of schizophrenics, it is generally accepted that this hypothesis is unlikely to be true.

- Explanations implicating **dopamine** have received more support. Schizophrenia is not caused by an excess of dopamine, but by the manner of its utilisation. Schizophrenics apparently have more numerous or densely packed receptor sites for dopamine.

- Cocaine and amphetamine stimulate dopamine receptors, producing schizophrenia-like symptoms in non-schizophrenics, and exacerbating the symptoms of diagnosed schizophrenics. Drugs which block dopamine receptors reduce schizophrenic symptoms.

- The **diathesis–stress model** proposes that schizophrenia is the result of an interaction between biological vulnerability and personally significant environmental stressors. The **vulnerability–stress model** specifies the genetically determined traits that can make a person vulnerable, such as hyperactivity and faulty information-processing.

- Schizophrenia's **positive (Type 1) symptoms** might have one cause (related to dopamine), whilst its **negative (Type 2)** symptoms might have some other cause (related to brain damage). Damage may be caused by oxygen deficits at birth. However, although there are several structural differences between schizophrenic and non-schizophrenic brains, these differences are modest with considerable overlap between the two populations.

- Schizophrenia might be a **neurodevelopmental disorder** in which the brain fails to develop normally. One cause might be a **viral infection** occurring during the second trimester of pregnancy when the brain forms crucial interconnections. However, the evidence concerning viral theories is inconclusive and sometimes contradictory.

## 2 Introduction and overview

*Mood* (or *affective*) *disorders* involve a prolonged and fundamental disturbance of mood and emotions. Mood is a pervasive and sustained emotional state that colours perceptions, thoughts and behaviours. At one extreme is *manic disorder* (or *mania*), characterised by wild, exuberant and unrealistic activity, and a flight of ideas or distracting thoughts. At the other is *depressive disorder*. Mania usually occurs in conjunction with depression and in such cases is called *bipolar disorder*. However, when mania occurs alone, the term bipolar is also used, the term *unipolar* being reserved for the experience of depression only. The term *manic–depressive* refers to both the unipolar and bipolar forms of affective disorder.

This chapter describes depression's characteristics and looks at some of the explanations for 'the common cold' (Seligman, 1973) of psychological problems.

## The characteristics of depression

By 'common cold', Seligman means that depression is the most common psychological problem people face. During the coming year, most of us will experience some symptoms of depression (Beck & Young, 1978). When a loved one dies or a relationship ends, depression is a normal reaction. Indeed, most psychologically healthy people occasionally 'get the blues' or 'feel down'. However, this usually passes fairly quickly. For a diagnosis of *clinical depression*, several characteristics need to have co-occurred for a period of time.

Unipolar depression can occur at any age, and may appear gradually or suddenly. In the United States, around 15 per cent of adults aged between 18 and 74 will experience serious depression. In Britain, the estimated figure is five per cent (SANE, 1993).

**Box 2.1** *The characteristics of clinical depression*

Clinical depression is defined by persistent low mood for at least two weeks, plus at least five of the following:

- poor appetite or weight loss or increased appetite or weight gain (a change of 0.5 kg per week over several weeks or 4.5 kg in a year when not dieting);
- difficulty in sleeping (*insomnia*) or sleeping longer than usual (*hypersomnia*);
- loss of energy or tiredness to the point of being unable to make even the simplest everyday decisions;
- an observable slowing down or agitation. In an attempt to discharge feelings of restlessness, people will often wring their hands, pace about or complain (*agitated depression*);
- a markedly diminished loss of interest or pleasure in activities that were once enjoyed;
- feelings of self-reproach or excessive or inappropriate guilt over real or imagined misdeeds. These may develop into *delusions* (see Chapter 1, page 3);
- complaints or evidence of diminished ability to think or concentrate;
- recurrent thoughts of death (not just a fear of dying), suicide, suicidal thoughts without a specific plan, or a suicide attempt or a specific plan for committing suicide.

(Adapted from Spitzer *et al.*, 1981)

Deeply embedded within psychiatric thinking is the distinction between *endogenous* and *exogenous* (or *reactive*) depression. Endogenous ('coming from within') was used to describe depression arising from biochemical disturbances in the brain. Exogenous ('coming from the outside') was used to describe depression occurring as a reaction (hence *reactive*) to stressful life experiences. However, this distinction is controversial and endogenous is now used to describe a cluster of symptoms, rather than the origins of the depression (Williams & Hargreaves, 1995).

**Box 2.2** *A typical case of depression*

A 55-year-old man has suffered from appetite loss and a 23 kg weight loss over the past six months. His appetite loss has been accompanied by a burning pain in his chest, back and abdomen, which he is convinced indicates a fatal abdominal cancer. He is withdrawn and isolated, unable to work, uninterested in friends and family, and unresponsive to their attempts to make him feel better. He awakes at 4 a.m. and is unable to fall back asleep. He claims to feel worse in the mornings and to improve slightly as the day wears on. He is markedly agitated and speaks of feelings of extreme unworthiness. He says that he would be better off dead and that he welcomes his impending demise from cancer.
(Adapted from Spitzer *et al.*, 1981)

As stated earlier, bipolar disorder is characterised by alternating periods of mania and depression, which seem to be unrelated to external events. Their duration and frequency vary from person to person. In some cases, manic and depressive episodes may be separated by long periods of normal functioning. In others, the episodes quickly follow one another. These unending cycles can be destructive for the people affected, their families and friends.

Bipolar disorder generally appears in the early 20s. Unlike depression (which is more prevalent in women: see pages 40–41), bipolar disorder is equally prevalent in men and women, although the disorder itself is much less common than depression. Interestingly, there is a disproportionately higher incidence of bipolar disorder among creative people (Jamison, 1989). For example, of 47 award-winning British writers and artists, 38 per cent were treated for the disorder (see also Post, 1994). In the general population, this figure is about one per cent.

**Box 2.3**  *A case of bipolar disorder*

For four months, Mrs S. has spent most of her time lying in bed. She appears sad and deep in thought and often states, 'I'm no good to anyone; I'm going to be dead soon'. She expresses feelings of hopelessness and listlessness and has difficulty concentrating. Suddenly, one day, her mood seems to be remarkably better. She is pleasant, verbalises more and appears somewhat cheerful. The following day, however, the rate of her speech is increased, she moves rapidly, shows a flight of ideas, and intrudes into everyone's activities. Over a couple of days, this activity increases to the point where she is unable to control her actions and attempts to break the furniture. (Adapted from Spitzer *et al.*, 1981)

# Explanations of depression

## The behavioural model

Behavioural approaches to depression focus on the role played by *reinforcement*. Ferster (1965) proposed that depression is a result of a reduction in reinforcement. Lewinsohn (1974) expanded Ferster's theory and proposed that certain events, such as the death of a loved one, induce depression because they reduce positive reinforcement.

Depressed people may spend less time in social activities. At least initially, this leads to concern and attention being paid by their friends. Lewinsohn argues that concern and attention *reinforces* the depressed behaviour. However, after a while this concern and attention wanes. Thus, reinforcement is reduced and this exacerbates the depression. The result is that the depressed individual is caught in a cycle from which escape is difficult.

Lewinsohn sees people lacking social skills as prime candidates for depression, because social ineptness is unlikely to bring reinforcement from others. Consequently, the socially unskilled individual may exhibit the form of passive behaviour characterising depression. MacPhillamy & Lewinsohn (1974) found that

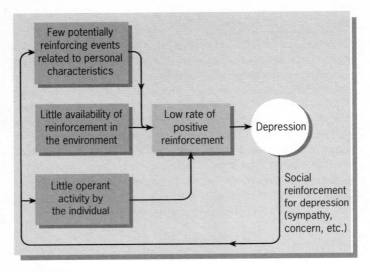

**Figure 2.1**  *Lewinsohn's model of depression*

depressed people report having fewer pleasant experiences than non-depressed people, and that greater depression was correlated with fewer pleasant experiences. However, whilst depression might *follow* a reduction in pleasant experiences, it could *precede* a reduction in those experiences, implying that people who become depressed might lower their participation in reinforcing events.

## Cognitive–behavioural model

Seligman's research represents a link between behavioural and cognitive perspectives. Seligman & Maier (1967) conducted an experiment in which dogs were restrained so that they could not avoid electric shocks. The dogs appeared to become passively resigned to the receipt of the shocks. Later, when they were placed in a situation in which they *could* escape the shocks, they made no attempt to do so. Seligman called this phenomenon *learned helplessness*.

**Box 2.4** *Learned helplessness*

Seligman argued that the dogs' behaviours (which included lethargy, sluggishness, and a loss of appetite) were similar to those exhibited by depressed humans. Depressed people (like dogs) learn from experience to develop an expectancy that their behaviours will be fruitless in bringing about an environmental change. When people feel helpless to influence their encounters with pleasurable and unpleasurable stimuli, they become depressed.

Seligman's account was criticised because it failed to address the issue of why some depressed people blame themselves for their depression, whilst others blame the external world, and the observation that depressed people tend to attribute their successes to luck rather than ability. Abramson *et al.*'s (1978) revised version of learned helplessness theory is based on the attributions or interpretations people make of their experiences. According to Abramson *et al.*, people who attribute failure to *internal* ('It's my fault'), *stable* ('It's going to last forever') and *global* ('It's going to affect everything I do') causes, and attribute successes to luck, are more likely to become depressed, because these factors lead to the perception that they are helpless to change things for the better. This *attributional style* derives from learning histories, especially in the family and at school.

Questionnaires assessing how people interpret adversities in life predict (to some degree) their future susceptibility to depression. However, although cognitions of helplessness often accompany depressive episodes, the cognitive pattern changes once the depressive episode ends. According to Gotlib & Colby (1995), people who were formerly depressed are actually no different from people who have never been depressed in terms of their tendencies to view negative events with an attitude of helpless resignation. This suggests that an attitude of helplessness could be a *symptom* rather than a *cause* of depression.

**Box 2.5**   *Beck's cognitive triad model*

A similar account to Seligman's is Beck's (1974) cognitive model of emotional disorders which states that:

'an individual's emotional response to an event or experience is determined by the conscious meaning placed on it'.

Beck believes that depression is based in self-defeating *negative beliefs* and *negative cognitive sets* (or tendencies to think in certain ways) that develop as a result of experience. Certain childhood and adolescence experiences (such as the loss of a parent or criticism from teachers) leads to the development of a *cognitive triad* consisting of three interlocking negative beliefs. These concern the *self*, the *world* and the *future*, and cause people to have a distorted and constricted outlook on life. The beliefs lead people to magnify bad, and minimise good, experiences. The cognitive triad is maintained by several kinds of distorted and illogical interpretations of real events that contribute to depression.

Some depressed people do describe their world in the ways outlined by Beck (White *et al.*, 1985). However, correlations do not imply causality, and it could be that depressed feelings and logical errors of thought are both caused by a third factor (perhaps a biochemical imbalance: see below). Additionally, the perception and recall of information in more negative terms might be the *result* of depression rather than the *cause* of it (Hammen, 1985).

Other research has looked at the role of *depressogenic schemata* (cognitions which may precipitate depression, and remain latent until activated by *stress*). Haaga & Beck (1992) have specified several types of stressor that may activate dysfunctional beliefs in people. For example, *sociotropic* individuals may be stressed by negative interactions with, or rejections by, others, whereas *autonomous* individuals may be stressed by a failure to reach personal goals. According to Teasdale's (1988) *differential activation hypothesis*, the increased accessibility of negative thoughts after an initial shift in mood may explain why some people suffer persistent rather than transient depression (Scott, 1994).

# Psychodynamic model

Psychodynamic approaches to mood disorders were first addressed by Abraham (1911). However, it was Freud (1917) who attempted to apply psychodynamic principles. He noted a similarity between the grieving that occurs when a loved one dies and the symptoms of depression. For Freud, depression was an excessive and irrational grief response to loss that evokes feelings associated with real or imagined loss of affection from the person on whom the individual was most dependent as a child.

Freud argued that both *actual losses* (such as the death of a loved one) and *symbolic losses* (such as the loss of a job or social prestige) lead us to re-experience parts of our childhood. Thus, depressed people become dependent and clinging or, in very extreme cases, regress to a childlike state. The greater the experience of loss in childhood, the greater the regression that occurred during adulthood. The evidence for Freud's account is, however, mixed. Some studies report that children who have lost a parent are particularly susceptible to depression later on (Roy, 1981). Others, however, have failed to find such a susceptibility (Lewinsohn & Hoberman, 1982).

Freud also argued that unresolved and repressed hostility towards one's parents was important. When loss is experienced, anger is evoked and is turned *inward* on the self because the outward expression of anger is unacceptable to the superego. This self-directed hostility creates feelings of guilt, unworthiness and despair, which may be so intense as to motivate *suicide* (the ultimate form of inward-directed aggression). Freud further believed that grief was complicated by inevitable mixed feelings. As well as affection, mourners are likely to have had at least occasionally angry feelings towards the deceased. However, these unacceptable feelings are also redirected towards the self, leading to lowered self-esteem and feelings of guilt.

Psychodynamic theorists see the occurrence of bipolar disorder as the result of the alternating dominance of personality by the superego (in the depressive phase of the disorder), which floods the individual with exaggerated ideas of wrong-doing and associated feelings of guilt and worthlessness, and the ego (in the manic phase), which attempts to defend itself by rebounding and asserting supremacy. As a response to the ego's excessive display, the superego dominates, resulting in feelings of guilt which again plunges the individual into depression.

---

**Box 2.6** *Weaknesses of the psychodynamic model's account of depression*

At least four reasons suggest that the psychodynamic model is inadequate in explaining mood disorders in general, and depression in particular. First, there is no direct evidence that depressed people interpret the death of a loved one as desertion or rejection of themselves (Davison & Neale, 1990). Second, if anger is turned inward, we would not expect depressed people to direct excessive amounts of hostility towards people who are close to them. This does, however, occur (Weissman & Paykel, 1974). Third, there is little evidence for a direct connection between early loss and the risk of depression in adult life (Crook & Eliot, 1980). Finally, since symbolic loss cannot be observed, this aspect of the theory cannot be experimentally assessed.

---

## Medical model
### Genetic influences
Based on the observation that mood disorders tend to run in families, a *genetic* basis for them has been proposed. According to Weissman (1987), people with first-degree relatives (relatives with whom an individual shares 50 per cent of his or her genes – parents and siblings) who have a mood disorder are ten times more likely to develop one than people with unaffected first-degree relatives. Allen (1976) has reported a higher average concordance rate for bipolar disorder in MZs (72 per cent: the highest for *any* mental disorder) than in DZs (14 per cent).

For major depression, the average concordance rate for MZs is 40 per cent and only 11 per cent for DZs (Allen, 1976). The fact that concordance rates for bipolar disorder and major depression differ suggests that, if genetic factors are involved, they are different for the two disorders. As noted in Chapter 1, however, the data from families and twins is limited by the fact that they usually share the same environment. However, as with schizophrenia, this problem has been at least partially overcome by adoption studies. Adopted children who later develop a mood disorder appear to be much more likely to have a biological parent who has a mood disorder, becomes alcoholic or commits suicide, even though the adopted children are raised in very different environments (Wender *et al.*, 1986).

---

**Box 2.7** *DNA markers and mood disorders*

DNA markers have been used to identify the gene or genes involved in mood disorders. This approach looks at the inheritance of mood disorders within high-risk families, and then searches for a DNA segment that is inherited along with a predisposition to develop the disorder. Egeland *et al.* (1987) studied 81 people from four high-risk families, all of whom were members of the Old Order Amish community in Pennsylvania. Fourteen were diagnosed as having a bipolar disorder, and all had specific genetic markers at the tip of chromosome 11. However, subsequent research has failed to replicate this finding in other populations in which bipolar disorder appears to be inherited.

Whilst these data do not invalidate those of Egeland *et al.*, other researchers have failed to support their findings when the analysis was extended to other Amish relatives (Kelsoe *et al.*, 1989). This suggests at least two possibilities: the gene for bipolar disorder may not actually be on chromosome 11, or several genes play a role, only one of which is on chromosome 11. The latter is supported by the observation that a gene on the X chromosome has also been implicated in bipolar disorder (Baron *et al.*, 1987).

Ogilvie *et al.* (1996) have shown that cells use a gene called SERT to make a serotonin transporter protein which plays an important role in the transmission of information between neurons. In most people, part of this gene (the *second intron*) contains ten or 12 repeating sections of DNA. However, in a significant number of people with depression, this part of the gene has only nine repeating sequences. The fact that serotonin is strongly implicated in depression (see below) and that newer anti-depressant drugs such as Prozac (see Chapter 72) interact with the serotonin transporter protein, offers one of the strongest hints yet that genes may be involved in depression.

### Biochemical influences

As mentioned in Chapter 1, genes act by directing biochemical events. Researchers have looked at the *biochemical processes* which may play a causal role in affective disorders. Research has linked these disorders to chemical imbalances in *serotonin* and *noradrenaline*. Schildkraut (1965) argued that too much noradrenaline at certain sites caused mania, whereas too little caused depression. Later research suggested that serotonin played a similar role.

Certainly, some evidence supports these proposals. For example, non-humans given drugs that diminish noradrenaline production become sluggish and inactive, two symptoms of depression (Wender & Klein, 1981). Similar effects occur when humans are given *reserpine*, used to treat high blood pressure. Additionally, drugs which are effective in reducing depression increase brain levels of noradrenaline and/or serotonin (Lemonick, 1997). *Iproniazid* (used to treat tuberculosis) produces elation and euphoria and increases noradrenaline and serotonin levels. Lithium carbonate (a treatment for mania) decreases noradrenaline and serotonin levels.

Research also indicates that depressed people's urine contains lower than normal levels of compounds produced when noradrenaline and serotonin are broken down by enzymes (Teuting *et al.*, 1981), suggesting lower than normal activity of noradrenaline and serotonin-secreting neurones in the brain. Abnormally high levels of noradrenaline compounds have been found in the urine of manic people (Kety, 1975), and the level of these compounds fluctuates in people with bipolar disorder (Bunney *et al.*, 1972).

---

**Box 2.8**  *The permissive amine theory of mood disorder*

Schildkraut's theory was weakened by the finding that whilst noradrenaline *and* serotonin are lower in depression, lower levels of serotonin are also found in mania. Thus, it cannot be a simple case of an excess or deficiency of these neurotransmitters that causes mania and depression. An attempt to reconcile these observations is Kety's *permissive amine theory of mood disorder* (noradrenaline and serotonin are examples of *biogenic amines*, hence the theory's name). According to Kety, serotonin plays a role in limiting noradrenaline levels. When serotonin levels are normal, so are noradrenaline levels, and only normal highs and lows are experienced. However, when serotonin is deficient, it cannot play its limiting role and so noradrenaline levels fluctuate beyond normal high and low levels, leading to mania and depression.

---

Whilst drugs that alleviate depression increase noradrenaline and serotonin levels, they do so only in the period immediately after taking the drug. Within a few days, the levels return to baseline. The problem for Kety's theory is that antidepressant effects do *not* occur during the period when transmitter levels are elevated. All anti-depressants take some time before they alleviate depression. This suggests that depression cannot be explained simply in terms of a change in neurotransmitter levels. It is more likely that the drugs act to reduce depression by increasing the *sensitivity* of receiving neurons, thereby allowing them to utilise limited neurotransmitter supplies in a more effective way (Sulser, 1979).

Additionally, antidepressant drugs are not always effective in reducing depression, not everyone suffering from depression shows reduced neurotransmitter levels, and not everyone displaying mania shows increased noradrenaline levels. Whilst it is likely that neurotransmitters play a role in mood disorders, these findings demonstrate that their exact role remains to be determined (Fields, 1991).

---

**Box 2.9** *Structural differences in the brains of depressives*

Part of the brain called the subgenual prefrontal cortex, which is located about 2½ inches (6 cm) behind the bridge of the nose, is known to play an important role in the control of emotion. In depressed people, it is eight per cent less active than in non-depressed people, and there is 40–50 per cent less tissue in the depressed. This deficit may result from a catastrophic loss of an as yet unknown subset of neurons by an also as yet unknown cause (Gorman, 1997).

---

### External factors and biochemical influences

Whilst the evidence suggests that affective disorders are heritable and that biochemical factors are involved, the exact cause-and-effect relationships remain to be established. If a gene is involved, its exact mode of transmission must be complex, given the variation in the severity and manner of the expression of mood disorders. Serotonin might act as the regulator, or serotonin and noradrenaline might play different roles in different types of mood disorders. Also, the possibility that neurotransmitter levels change as a result of the mood disorder rather than being its cause cannot be excluded. For example, environmental stimuli may cause depression which causes biochemical changes in the brain. Noradrenaline levels are lower in dogs in whom learned helplessness has been induced (Miller *et al.*, 1977). The dogs did not inherit such levels, but acquired them as a result of their experiences.

Two sub-types of *seasonal affective disorder* of particular interest are *summer depression* (associated with loss of appetite, weight and sleep) and *winter depression* (associated with increased weight, sleep and appetite for carbohydrate foods). Wurtman & Wurtman (1989) have argued that summer depression is associated with deficiencies in serotonin levels, whilst winter depression is almost certainly caused by the desynchronisation of the rhythm of *melatonin* as the result of decreasing natural light exposure in winter (Wehr & Rosenthal, 1989). In summer depression, a mechanism other than decreasing light exposure must play a role.

Laboratory studies of non-humans have shown that changes in magnetic field exposure, which alters the direction of the magnetic field, are correlated with decreased melatonin synthesis and serotonin production (Rudolph *et al.*, 1993). On the basis of these findings, Kay (1994) hypothesises that geomagnetic storms might partly account for the bimodal annual distribution of depression (that is, summer *and* winter depression). Kay reported a 36 per cent increase in male hospital admissions for depression in the second week following such storms, and believes that the effects of geomagnetic storms on melatonin synthesis and serotonin production are the same in humans and non-humans.

Bush (cited in Whittell, 1995) has investigated the high suicide rate in the remote Alaskan hinterland, where suicide levels among the state's 15–24 year olds are six times the USA average. Bush argues for a link between the *aurora borealis* (or Northern lights), a source of changes in geomagnetism, and electrical activity in the brain. Additionally, the British finding that new mothers and pregnant women are 60 per cent more likely to suffer depression if they live near high-voltage electricity cables than those who do not, coupled with clusters of suicides in people living close to such cables, suggests that electromagnetic fields *might* be involved in this disorder (Westhead, 1996).

Whatever seasonal depression's causes, the anti-depressant drug *sertraline* is effective, at least in winter depression, and produces even better effects than *phototherapy*, which is inconvenient, costly and associated with headaches and eye strain (Syal, 1997).

# Sex differences in depression

According to Cochrane (1995), when all relevant factors are controlled for, depression contributes most highly to the overall rate of treatment for mental disorders in women, who are two to three times more likely than men to become clinically depressed (Williams & Hargreaves, 1995).

Several factors may account for the sex difference. These include hormonal fluctuations associated with the menstrual cycle, childbirth, the menopause, taking oral contraceptives, brain chemistry and diet.

---

**Box 2.10**   *Brain biochemistry and diet*

According to Diksic *et al.* (cited in Highfield, 1997b), serotonin is made by men's brain stems at a rate 52 per cent higher than in women. This could be due to the way men and women develop. One possibility is that dieting during the teenage years might alter brain biochemistry. Smith *et al.* (1997) found that women experienced symptoms of depression when *tryptophan*, a protein component, was removed from their diets. Tryptophan is an amino-acid precursor of serotonin, and even a standard 1000-calorie carbohydrate-restricted diet can lower blood plasma levels of it enough to alter serotonin function.

---

The evidence concerning hormonal and other factors is, however, weak. For example, although one in ten women who have just given birth are sufficiently depressed to need medical or psychological help, no specific causal hormonal abnormality has been identified. It is just as plausible to suggest that social factors (such as the adjustment to a new role) are as important as any proposed physical factors (Callaghan & O'Carroll, 1993; Murray, 1995).

Cochrane (1995) has summarised non-biological explanations of women's greater susceptibility to depression. For example, girls are very much more likely to be sexually abused than boys, and victims of abuse are at least twice as likely to experience clinical depression in adulthood, compared with non-abused individuals. Abuse alone, then, might explain the sex difference. An alternative account is based on the fact that the sex difference is greatest between the ages of 20 and 50, the years when marriage, child-bearing, motherhood and the *empty nest syndrome* will be experienced by a majority of women.

Although women are increasingly becoming part of the labour force, being a full-time mother and wife, having no employment outside of the home, and lacking an intimate and confiding relationship, are increasingly being seen as risk factors for depression (Brown & Harris, 1978). The acceptance of a traditional female gender role may contribute to *learned helplessness* (see page 31), because the woman sees herself as having little control over her life.

Depression may be seen as a *coping strategy* that is available to women (Cochrane, 1983). Not only is it more acceptable for women to admit to psychological problems, but such problems may represent a means of changing an intolerable situation. As Callaghan & O'Carroll (1993) have observed:

'Unhappiness about their domestic, social, and political circumstances lies at the root of many women's concerns. This unhappiness must not be medicalised and regarded as a "female malady"'.

## Conclusions

Like schizophrenia, depression is a serious mental disorder with many distinct characteristics. Several explanations have been advanced to explain the disorder. All have received support, although we are still some way from a single accepted explanation for depression.

# Summary

- At one extreme of **mood/affective disorder** is manic disorder/mania. At the other is **depressive disorder**. Mania on its own or, more usually, in conjunction with depression, is called **bipolar disorder**. **Unipolar disorder** refers to depression only. **Manic–depression** refers to both unipolar and bipolar disorders.

- Depression is the most common mental disorder and can be a response to certain life events or just part of 'everyday life'. To be diagnosed as **clinically depressed**, a person must display persistent low mood for at least two weeks, plus at least five other symptoms identified in diagnostic criteria.

- The traditional distinction between **endogenous** and **exogenous/reactive** depression is controversial. Endogenous no longer denotes depression's origins, but refers to a cluster of symptoms. Depression can occur at any age and is more common in women. Bipolar disorder generally appears in the early 20s and is equally prevalent in men and women.

- **Behavioural** explanations of depression focus on the role played by a reduction in **positive reinforcement**. Cognitive–behavioural accounts use the concept of **learned helplessness** to explain depression. However, learned helplessness on its own cannot account for depressed people's **attributional styles**.

- According to Beck's **cognitive model**, depression is based in self-defeating **negative beliefs** and **cognitive sets**. The **cognitive triad** leads people to exaggerate their bad experiences and minimise their good experiences.

- **Depressogenic schemata** may be activated by rejections from others (in **sociotropic** individuals) or a failure to reach personal goals (in **autonomous** individuals). The **differential activation hypothesis** is an attempt to explain persistent and transient depression.

- The **psychodynamic model** proposes that both **actual** and **symbolic losses** cause us to re-experience parts of childhood, and depression may involve a regression to a childlike dependency. However, the psychodynamic model is inadequate in explaining mood disorders in general and depression in particular.

- Because mood disorders run in families, they might have a **genetic** basis. This is supported by the higher concordance rate in MZs than DZs. DNA markers have been used to identify the gene(s) involved, although the data are equivocal in this respect. The SERT gene offers the strongest evidence yet for a genetic basis to mood disorders.

- Lower than normal levels of activity in **serotonin-** and **noradrenaline-secreting** neurons may be a causal factor in depression. Kety's **permissive amine theory** describes their interaction, but is inconsistent with some evidence. Whilst it is likely that neurotransmitters play a role in mood disorders, exactly what it is remains to be discovered.

- Seasonal variations in the incidence of depression are well-established. **Winter depression** is almost certainly caused by the desynchronisation of **melatonin** as a result of decreasing natural light exposure in winter. **Summer depression** is more difficult to explain. Geomagnetic factors may be involved in both forms of depression, by influencing melatonin synthesis and serotonin production.

- Sex differences in depression have been explained both in biological and psychological terms. Biological explanations implicate the menstrual cycle, childbirth, the menopause, oral contraceptives, and the influence of dieting on brain biochemistry. Psychological explanations implicate sexual abuse, the stress associated with marriage, childbearing, motherhood, and the 'empty nest syndrome'. Depression may even be a **coping strategy** for women.

## 3

## Introduction and overview

Researchers generally agree that some anxiety is *biologically adaptive* because it produces enhanced vigilance and a more realistic appraisal of a situation, allowing us to develop appropriate coping responses. Some people, however, experience anxiety that is so overwhelming it interferes with normal everyday functioning.

*Anxiety disorders* is a category in DSM-IV that is subsumed by the category *neurotic, stress-related* and *somatoform disorders* in ICD-10. DSM-IV recognises four types of anxiety disorder. These are *panic disorders* and *generalised anxiety disorder, phobic disorders* (which ICD-10 calls *phobic anxiety disorders*), *obsessive–compulsive disorder* and *post-traumatic stress disorder* (which ICD-10 includes under the heading *stress* and *adjustment disorders*). This chapter describes the characteristics associated with each of the four disorders identified by DSM-IV and examines explanations for their causes.

## Panic disorder (PD) and Generalised anxiety disorder (GAD)

Anxiety is a general feeling of dread or apprehensiveness typically accompanied by various physiological reactions, including increased heart rate, rapid and shallow breathing, sweating, muscle tension and a dryness of the mouth. In both *panic disorder* (PD) and *generalised anxiety disorder* (GAD), the anxiety is 'free-floating', and occurs in the absence of any obvious anxiety-provoking object or situation. Thus, a person experiences anxiety but does not know why.

The physiological reactions accompanying unpredictable and repeated anxiety and panic attacks are similar to those that occur during a heart attack. Other reactions include chest pain and a tingling in the hands or feet, and it is common for people experiencing panic disorder to actually *believe* they are having a heart attack. Other symptoms include *derealisation* (the feeling that the world is not real) and *depersonalisation* (the loss of a sense of personal identity, manifested as a feeling of detachment from the body). Panic attacks can last for a few minutes to several hours. Although they usually occur during wakefulness, they can occur during sleep (Dilsaver, 1989).

---

**Box 3.1** *A typical case of panic disorder*

When this 38-year-old man experienced intense anxiety, it seemed as if he were having a heart seizure. He had chest pains and heart palpitations, numbness and shortness of breath, and felt a strong need to breathe in air. He reported that in the midst of this he developed a tight feeling over his eyes and could only see objects directly in front of him. He also feared he would not be able to swallow.

The anxiety's intensity was very frightening, and on two occasions his wife had rushed him to hospital because he was in a state of panic, sure that his heart was going to stop beating. His symptoms were relieved after an injection of tranquilliser medication. He began to note where doctors' offices and hospitals were wherever he happened to be, and became extremely anxious if medical help were not close by.

(Adapted from Leon, 1990)

---

PD may be so terrifying that a person experiencing it can be driven to suicide. In many cases, it is accompanied by *agoraphobia*, a fear of finding oneself in a situation from which escape is difficult or where help is not available should a panic attack occur (see page 48). Because PD occurs without any apparent cause, sufferers also experience *anticipatory anxiety*, a worry about when the next attack will occur and the avoidance of situations in which it has occurred.

GAD is characterised by persistent high levels of anxiety and worry about things, accompanied by the physical sensations associated with PD. However, although GAD's physical sensations are more persistent than in PD, they are less intense. The physical, cognitive and emotional problems caused by GAD lead people experiencing it to become tired, irritable, socially inept and to have difficulty functioning effectively.

## Explanations of PD and GAD

As mentioned previously, some people develop anticipatory anxiety and actively avoid situations in which they believe PD will occur. The cues associated with situations in which anxiety is aroused can lead to it being experienced (Clark, 1993). Avoidance is *reinforced* by a reduction in the disorder's fear component. However, the *origins* of all cases of PD probably cannot be explained in conditioning terms, and it is likely that classical conditioning increases PD's severity rather than causes it (Sue *et al.*, 1994).

---

**Box 3.2** *Catastrophising cognitions*

Certain cognitions can act as *internal triggers* for PD (Belfer & Glass, 1992). Clark (1993) proposes that the core disturbance in panic is an abnormality in thinking. When external or internal stressors cause increased physiological activity, this is noticed but interpreted in catastrophic ways (such as 'I am having a heart attack'). This leads to even more physiological activity, which only confirms the catastrophic thinking, and so a *positive feedback loop* between cognitions and bodily activity occurs. Although some evidence supports this proposal, sufferers often report being unaware of particular thoughts during a panic attack. It is also unclear why catastrophic thoughts *should* be characteristic of the disorder.

---

The psychodynamic model sees GAD as the result of unacceptable unconscious conflicts blocked by the ego. These are powerful enough to produce constant tension and apprehension, but since they are unconscious, the person is unaware of the anxiety's source. To defend ourselves, we try to repress the impulses, but our defences are occasionally weakened and PD occurs. Alternatively, PD could represent unresolved *separation anxiety*, which may be experienced later in life when a threat of separation is either perceived or actually occurs.

There might be a *genetic* component in PD and GAD. Around 40 per cent of first-degree relatives of PD sufferers have the disorder themselves (Balon *et al.*, 1989), and there is a higher concordance rate in MZs than in DZs (Slater & Shields, 1969). Although environmental factors cannot be ruled out, what might be inherited is a predisposition towards anxiety in the form of a highly reactive ANS (Eysenck, 1967). For example, some people with GAD demonstrate *autonomic lability*, that is, they are more easily aroused by environmental stimuli.

Lesch *et al.* (cited in Highfield, 1996) have shown that neuroticism levels are correlated with two versions of a gene responsible for transporting serotonin. One of these leads to more serotonin and neuroticism, and the other to less of these. However, the gene accounts for only about four per cent of the total variation in anxiety, so other factors clearly cannot be ruled out. Papp *et al.* (1993) argue that PD is triggered by a dysfunction in receptors that monitor oxygen levels in the blood. By incorrectly informing the brain that the levels are low, fear of suffocation and hyperventilation result. PD is accompanied by an elevated blood level of *lactic acid*, a by-product of muscular activity. In *biological challenge tests*, sodium lactate is given to people with PD and, in most of them, a panic attack occurs (George & Ballenger, 1992).

This may be because the *locus coeruleus*, a brain structure associated with anxiety, is overly sensitive to anything that is *anxiogenic* (anxiety-inducing). However, the results of biological challenge tests are influenced by *expectations*. People informed they will experience pleasant sensations report less anxiety than those informed they will experience unpleasant sensations. Even if biological factors do play a role, then, it is likely that cognitive factors can modify them (Sue *et al.*, 1994).

# Phobic disorders

Being afraid of something that might objectively cause us harm is a normal reaction. However, some people show strong, persistent and *irrational* fears of, and desires to avoid, particular objects, activities or situations. When such behaviour interferes with normal everyday functioning, a person has a phobia. Encountering the phobic stimulus results in intense anxiety. Although a phobic usually acknowledges that the anxiety is out of proportion to the actual danger the phobic stimulus poses, this does little to reduce the fear, and he or she is highly motivated to avoid it.

DSM-IV identifies three categories of phobia. These are *agoraphobia*, *social phobia* and *specific phobias*. *Agoraphobia* is a fear of open spaces but, as mentioned earlier (see page 45), it typically involves a fear of being in situations from which escape may be difficult or where help is unavailable. In extreme cases, agoraphobics become 'prisoners' trapped in their own homes and dependent on others. Agoraphobia accounts for around 10–50 per cent of all phobias, and most agoraphobics are women. The phobia typically occurs in early adulthood.

*Social phobia* was identified as an entity in the UK in 1970, but not included in DSM until 1980 (Menninger, 1995). It is an intense and excessive fear of being in a situation in which being scrutinised by others is a possibility. It is also characterised by the fear that, in a particular situation, one will act in a way humiliating or embarrassing for the self or others (see Box 3.4, page 50).

A *specific phobia* is an extreme fear of a specific object (such as spiders) or situation (such as being in an enclosed space). The phobias identified in Box 3.3 are all specific phobias. Taken together, specific phobias are the most common phobic disorders, but also the *least disruptive*. Phobias are the most common type of anxiety disorder, and whilst there are sex differences in the likelihood of developing agoraphobia or social phobia, there are no such differences for most of the specific phobias. Specific

**Box 3.3** *Some varieties of phobias*

Acrophobia (high places)
Ailurophobia (cats)
Algophobia (pain)
Anthropophobia (men)
Aquaphobia (water)
Arachnophobia (spiders)
Astraphobia (storms, thunder, lightning)
Belonophobia (needles)
Cancerophobia (cancer)
Claustrophobia (enclosed spaces)
Cynophobia (dogs)
Hematophobia (blood)
Monophobia (being alone)
Mysophobia (contamination or germs)
Nycotophobia (darkness)
Ochlophobia (crowds)
Ophidiophobia (snakes)
Pathophobia (disease)
Pyrophobia (fire)
Siderophobia (railways)
Taphophobia (being buried alive)
Thanatophobia (death)
Triskaidekaphobia (thirteen)
Xenophobia (strangers)
Zoophobia (animals or a specific animal)

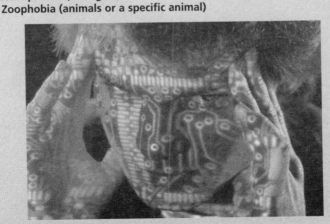

**Figure 3.1** *Technophobia is a feeling of fear or frustration experienced by people unfamiliar with modern digital and computer technology*

phobias usually develop in childhood, but can occur at any time. The *nosophobias* (or 'illness and injury' phobias, such as can-cerophobia and thanatophobia) tend to occur in middle age.

---

**Box 3.4** *Types of social phobia*

Three types of social phobia can be distinguished. *Performance social phobia* is characterised by excessive anxiety over activities like public speaking or being in a restaurant. In *limited interactional* social phobia, anxiety occurs only in specific situations, such as inter-acting with an authority figure. *Generalised* social phobia involves displaying anxiety in most social situations. Social phobia accounts for around ten per cent of all phobias and, like agoraphobia, most social phobics are women. Social phobia typically arises in adoles-cence.

**Figure 3.2** *Having to make a speech in front of any kind of audience is likely to induce some degree of anxiety in most people. As a social phobia, anxiety over public speaking is an intense and excessive fear of being exposed to scrutiny by other people; it is an example of performance social phobia*

---

**Box 3.5**  *Popeye phobia*

A three-year-old girl suddenly developed recurrent bronchitis which got worse when she attended nursery school. The trouble was traced to the slippers of a boy in the same class. Every time the girl saw them she began to retch, cough and become upset. The slippers sported a picture of Popeye, the cartoon character. Even the mention of his name provoked coughing. The girl had seen a cartoon of Popeye at her friend's house and became frightened of him. Following behaviour therapy, the girl recovered.
(Based on Murray, 1997)

## Explanations of phobic disorders

The psychodynamic model sees phobias as the *surface* expression of a much deeper conflict between the id, ego and superego, which has its origins in childhood. Freud (1909) described the case of 'Little Hans', a five-year-old boy, whose phobia of horses prevented him from leaving his house. Freud believed that phobias were expressions of unacceptable wishes, fears and fantasies displaced from their original, internal source onto some external object or situation that can be easily avoided. Freud saw Hans's fear of horses as an expression of anxieties related to his Oedipal complex. Since Hans unconsciously feared and hated his father (whom he perceived to be a rival for his mother's affection), he displaced this fear onto horses, which could be avoided more easily than his father.

Freud's explanation was challenged by the behavioural model. Hans's phobic response *only* occurred in the presence of a large horse pulling a heavily loaded cart at high speed, and his phobia had developed *after* Hans had witnessed a terrible accident involving a horse pulling a cart at high speed. Phobias *can* be classically conditioned (Watson & Rayner, 1920), and the behavioural model's interpretation of Hans's phobia is at least as plausible as Freud's.

Wolpe (1969) has argued that classical conditioning explains the development of *all* phobias. Certainly, the pairing of a neutral stimulus with a frightening experience is acknowledged by some phobics as marking their phobias' onset. Moreover, the *resilient* nature of some phobias (their *resistance* to *extinction*) can also be explained in conditioning terms.

---

**Box 3.6**  *The two-process theory of phobias*

According to Mowrer's (1947) *two-process* or *two-factor theory*, phobias are acquired through classical conditioning (factor 1) and maintained through operant conditioning (factor 2), because the avoidance of the phobic stimulus and the associated reduction in anxiety is *negatively reinforcing* (although Rachman's, 1984, *safety signal hypothesis* sees avoidance as being motivated by the positive feelings of safety).

---

However, the fact that some phobics cannot recall any traumatic experiences and that profound trauma does not inevitably lead to a phobia developing is difficult for the behavioural model to explain. Research also indicates that certain classes of stimuli (such as snakes) can more easily be made a conditioned stimulus than others (such as flowers).

---

**Box 3.7**  *Preparedness*

Rosenhan & Seligman (1984) propose an interaction between genetic and conditioning factors that biologically predisposes us to acquire phobias towards certain classes of stimuli. According to the concept of *preparedness* or *prepared conditioning*, we are genetically prepared to fear things that were sources of danger in our evolutionary past. Hugdahl & Öhman (1977) and Menzies (cited in Hunt, 1995) have shown that, in laboratory studies, people are more 'prepared' to acquire fear reactions to some stimuli than others. However, such studies do *not* demonstrate biological preparedness. Because we live in a society in which many people react negatively to certain animals, learning experiences rather than genetic factors might prepare us to fear these stimuli.

---

According to Rachman (1977), many phobias are acquired through information transmitted by *observation* and *instruction*. Although preparedness for direct conditioning does not seem to be relevant, a preparedness for observational and instructional learning is possible (Murray & Foote, 1979). Slater & Shields' (1969) observation of a 41 per cent concordance rate amongst MZs and only a four per cent rate amongst DZs is suggestive of a genetic role. However, without data relating to MZs reared *apart*, the role played by genetic factors is unclear. A relationship might also exist between a person's arousal level and the likelihood of a phobia developing, although the finding that high levels of physiological arousal are not associated with specific phobias casts doubt on such a proposal's generality (Tallis, 1994).

## Obsessive–compulsive disorder

As its name suggests, in *obsessive–compulsive disorder* (OCD) the profound anxiety is reflected in obsessions and compulsions. *Obsessions* are recurrent thoughts or images that do not feel voluntarily controlled and are experienced as senseless or repugnant. *Compulsions* are irresistible urges to engage in repetitive behaviours performed according to rituals or rules as a way of reducing or preventing the discomfort associated with some future undesirable event.

All of us have thoughts and behaviour patterns that are repeated, but these would only be a problem if they caused personal distress or interfered with daily life. OCD has recently undergone a dramatic change in status (Tallis, 1994, 1995). Once regarded as a rare neurosis, it now occupies a central position in clinical psychology and contemporary psychiatry. In the United States, OCD is the fourth most common psychological problem. In Britain, an estimated one to one-and-a-half million people suffer from it. Females are slightly more likely to be OCD sufferers and the disorder usually begins in young adulthood, and sometimes childhood.

**Box 3.8**   *Characteristics of obsessive thought*

Frequently, obsessive thoughts take the form of violent images, such as killing oneself or others. However, they can take other forms. The four most common obsessional characteristics are *impaired control over mental processes* (such as repetitive thoughts of a loved one's death), *concern of losing control over motor behaviours* (such as killing someone), *contamination* (by, for example, germs) and *checking behaviours* (such as concern over whether a door has been locked). Whatever form they take, the thoughts cannot be resisted and are unpleasant for the sufferer (Sanavio, 1988).

Often, compulsions arise from obsessions. For example, a person persistently thinking about contamination by germs may develop complex rituals for avoiding contamination, which are repeated until the person is satisfied that cleanliness has been achieved (even if the hands become raw as a result of being washed over 500 times a day: Davison & Neale, 1990).

**Box 3.9**   *A case of obsessive thoughts leading to compulsive behaviour*

Shirley K., a 23-year-old housewife, complained of frequent attacks of headaches and dizziness. During the preceding three months, she had been disturbed by recurring thoughts that she might harm her two-year-old son either by stabbing or choking him (the obsessive thought). She constantly had to go to his room, touch the boy and feel him breathe in order to reassure herself that he was still alive (the compulsive act), otherwise she became unbearably anxious. If she read a report in the daily paper of the murder of a child, she would become agitated, since this reinforced her fear that she, too, might act on her impulse.
(From Goldstein & Palmer, 1975)

Shakespeare's character Lady Macbeth, who acquired a hand-washing compulsion after helping her husband murder the King of Scotland, is perhaps the most famous fictional OCD sufferer. The late billionaire Howard Hughes, who wore gloves all the time, walked on clean paper, bathed repeatedly and refused to see people for fear of being contaminated by them, is perhaps the most well-known non-fictional sufferer, along with Charles Darwin, Martin Luther and John Bunyan (Bennett, 1997). Compulsives recognise that their behaviours are senseless, yet if prevented from engaging in them, they experience intense anxiety which is reduced only when the compulsive ritual is carried out (Hodgson & Rachman, 1972).

## Explanations of OCD

Comings & Comings' (1987) finding that people with OCD often have first-degree relatives with some sort of anxiety disorder suggests a genetic basis to OCD. However, the finding that in over half of the families of an OCD sufferer, members become actively involved in the rituals (Tallis, 1994), indicates the potential influence of *learning* (and supports the behavioural model). This might be particularly applicable to OCD's development in childhood: children with a parent who engages in ritualistic behaviour may see such behaviour as the norm (see below).

Evidence suggests that people with OCD show a different pattern of brain activity compared with non-OCD controls, in the form of increased metabolic activity in the left hemisphere's frontal lobe. When drugs are given which reduce this activity, the symptoms of OCD decline (McGuire *et al.*, 1994). However, whether OCD is a consequence of increased activity, a cause of it or merely a correlate is not yet known (Tallis, 1995). The fact that OCD can be treated using drugs which increase serotonin's availability indicates that a deficiency of that neurotransmitter might be implicated in it.

According to the psychodynamic model, obsessions are *defence mechanisms* that serve to occupy the mind and displace more threatening thoughts. Laughlin (1967), for example, sees the intrusion of obsessive thoughts as preventing the arousal of anxiety:

**'by serving as a more tolerable substitute for a subjectively less welcome thought or impulse'.**

Certainly, something like this might be practised by athletes who 'psych themselves up' before a competitive event and, from a psychodynamic perspective (and indeed from a cognitive perspective), this might function to exclude self-defeating doubts and thoughts. However, it is hard to see what thoughts of killing someone (which, as noted in Box 3.8, is one of the more common obsessional thoughts) are a more tolerable substitute for.

The behavioural model sees OCD as a way of reducing anxiety. If a particular thought or behaviour reduces anxiety, then it should (because it is reinforcing) become more likely to occur. This *anxiety-reduction hypothesis* explains the maintenance of OCD, but does not explain the disorder's development. However, the *superstition hypothesis* does.

---

**Box 3.10**   *The superstition hypothesis*

Skinner (1948) argued that what we call 'superstition' develops as a result of a chance association between a behaviour and a reinforcer. In Skinner's experiments, pigeons were given food at regular intervals irrespective of their behaviour. After a while, they displayed idiosyncratic movements, presumably because these were the movements they were making when the food was given.

The superstition hypothesis can account for many compulsive rituals (O'Leary & Wilson, 1975). Amongst soccer players, for example, many superstitious behaviours exist. These include always being last onto the pitch and putting the left sock on before the right. Such behaviours may occur because, in the past, they were associated with success. If such rituals are not permitted, anxiety is aroused. However, whilst chance associations between behaviours and reinforcers might explain the persistence of some *behaviours*, the development of intrusive *thoughts* is much more difficult for the behavioural model to explain.

---

## Post-traumatic stress disorder

During the First World War, many soldiers experienced *shell shock* (a shock-like state which followed the traumatic experiences of prolonged combat). Prior to being described as a clinical condition, it had been taken as a symptom of cowardice and sometimes resulted in summary trial and execution. In World War II, *combat exhaustion* was used to describe a similar reaction, characterised by terror, agitation or apathy, and insomnia.

Today, the term *post-traumatic stress disorder* (PTSD) is used to describe an anxiety disorder occurring in response to an extreme psychological or physical trauma outside the range of normal human experience (Thompson, 1997). As well as war, such traumas include a physical threat to one's self or family, witnessing other people's deaths, and being involved in a natural or human-made disaster. In Britain, several disasters associated with PTSD have been extensively researched. These include the Piper Alpha oil rig disaster, the bombing of the PanAm airliner that crashed at Lockerbie, and the death of over 90 spectators at the Hillsborough football ground.

---

**Box 3.11** *Children and PTSD*

The capsize of the cross-channel ferry *The Herald of Free Enterprise* in Zeebrugge has also been extensively researched. Studies of those who survived the disaster have shown that even very young children can be emotionally upset by such a trauma. Yule (1993), for example, reports that child survivors of recent disasters show PTSD's characteristic symptoms, including distressing recollections of the event, avoidance of reminders, and signs of increased physiological arousal, manifested as sleep disturbances and poor concentration.

Often, these children do not confide their distress to parents or teachers for fear of upsetting them. Consequently, their school work is affected and they are often thrown off their educational career course. However, when asked sympathetically and straightforwardly, they usually share their reactions. Other research has confirmed that children can experience PTSD. Pynoos *et al.* (1993) found a strong correlation between children's proximity to the epicentre of the 1988 Armenian earthquake and the overall severity of the core components of PTSD, with girls reporting more persistent anxiety than boys.

PTSD may occur immediately following a traumatic experience or weeks, months and even years later. In the Vietnam war, there were relatively few cases of shell shock or combat fatigue, probably because of the rapid turnover of soldiers in and out of the combat zone. However, on their return home, soldiers found it more difficult to adjust to civilian life than did those in the two World Wars.

As well as tiredness, apathy, depression, social withdrawal and nightmares, veterans reported *flashbacks* of events they had witnessed or participated in. They also showed *hyperalertness*, exaggerated startle reactions and felt guilty that they had survived but others had not. Like some people experiencing PTSD, they also reported using alcohol, drugs or violence to try to curb the disturbing symptoms (as have the survivors of *The Herald of Free Enterprise* disaster: Joseph *et al.*, 1993). Many veterans also cut themselves off from society to escape the sense of not being able to fit in as a result of their experiences.

One civilian disaster causing PTSD in those who survived it was the collision between two jumbo jets that killed 582 passengers in Tenerife in 1977. A combination of environmental and human factors led to a Dutch jumbo jet colliding with an American airliner. Many passengers were killed instantly, but some survived.

---

**Box 3.12**   *A case of post-traumatic stress disorder*

Martin lost his wife and blames himself for her death, because he sat stunned and motionless for some 25 seconds after the Dutch jumbo jet hit. He saw nothing but fire and smoke in the aisles, but roused himself and led his wife to a jagged hole above and behind his seat. Martin climbed out onto the wing and reached down and took hold of his wife's hand, but 'an explosion from within literally blew her out of my hands and pushed me back and down onto the wing'. He reached the runway, turned to go back after her, but the plane blew up seconds later.

Five months later, Martin was depressed and bored, had 'wild dreams', a short temper and became easily confused and irritated.

'What I saw there will terrify me forever,' he says. He told the psychologist who interviewed him that he avoided television and movies, because he couldn't know when a frightening scene would appear. (Adapted from Perlberg, 1979)

Hunt (1997) has studied apparent PTSD amongst people in their 60s and 70s evidently disturbed by their experiences in World War II. This is hardly surprising if it is assumed that they have been bothered *continuously* since the war. However, this assumption appears to be false, as most survivors got on with their lives, raised families and so on (Bender, 1995). For some reason, the memories seem to be coming back to disturb them now that they have retired (see below).

## Explanations of PTSD

Unlike other anxiety disorders, PTSD's origins can be explained largely, if not exclusively, in *environmental* terms. Whilst phobics or sufferers of OCD tend not to have common background factors, all PTSD sufferers share the experience of a profoundly traumatising event or events, even though these may be different from one another in other ways.

*Classical conditioning* is involved in PTSD (Kolb, 1987). Sufferers often show reactions to stimuli which were present at the time of the trauma. Hunt (1997), for example, interviewed veterans of the Normandy landings in World War II around the time of the fiftieth anniversary events in 1994. Many reported still being troubled by their memories of the war in general, but in particular were adversely affected by specific memories which had been revived by the anniversary commemorations.

As with phobias, however, classical conditioning cannot be the only mechanism involved, since not everyone who is exposed to a traumatic event develops PTSD. Green (1994) reports that PTSD develops in about 25 per cent of those who experience potentially traumatic events, although the range is quite large being about 12 per cent for accidents and 80 per cent for rape, with a *dose–effect relationship* between the stressor's severity and the degree of consequent psychological distress. Presumably, individual differences in how people perceive events as well as the *recovery environment* (such as support groups) also play an influential role.

Paton (1992), for example, found that relief workers at Lockerbie reported differences between what they expected to find and what they actually encountered, and that this was a source of stress. This was also reported by Dixon *et al.* (1993) in their study of PTSD amongst 'peripheral' victims of the *Herald of Free Enterprise* disaster. For relief workers, then, some way of increasing predictability (and hence control) that would minimise the differences between what is expected and what is observed, would be useful. Amongst the Normandy veterans, Hunt (1997) found that support systems, in the form of comradeship, were *still* important and were used by veterans as a means of coping with the traumatic memories (and often the physical consequences) of their war experiences.

The return of memories many years after a traumatic event suggests that keeping busy with socially valued life roles enables a person to *avoid* processing the traumatic memories. The unfortunate consequence of this, however, is that memories do not get integrated into a person's views about the world. To resolve the discrepancy, Bender (1995) suggests that people must process the traumatic experience and integrate it into their world views. In conditioning terms, thinking about the traumatic event would lead to *extinction* of the responses associated with it.

Although it is likely that social/psychological factors cause PTSD's onset, researchers are still interested in understanding the associated *biological processes*. The observation of similarities between PTSD and withdrawal from opioid drugs, and the finding that stress-induced analgesia can be reversed by *naloxone*

**Figure 3.3** *Despite being trained to deal with emergency situations, members of the emergency services cannot be prepared for major disasters, such as the Lockerbie, Hillsborough and* Herald of Free Enterprise *disasters. Police involved in the 1989 Hillsborough disaster were awarded (in 1996) substantial financial compensation for the 'mental injury' they suffered (post-traumatic stress disorder) and can be considered peripheral victims of the disaster*

(which reverses morphine's pharmacological action) in PTSD combat victims exposed to a combat movie, suggests that PTSD involves *disturbed opioid function* (van der Kolk *et al.*, 1989). Krystal *et al.* (1989) have proposed that the locus coeruleus acts as an 'alarm centre' and plays a pivotal role in PTSD's genesis. In support of this, drugs which are effective in treating PTSD also prevent the development of *learned helplessness* in non-humans exposed to inescapable shock (see Chapter 2, page 31) when these drugs are infused directly into the locus coeruleus (Davidson, 1992).

# Conclusions

This chapter has examined the characteristics of anxiety disorders and explanations of them. Some explanations are more powerful than others, depending on the anxiety disorder. As with the disorders considered in Chapters 1 and 2, however, there is still much debate about how anxiety disorders can best be explained.

# Summary

- Mild/moderate anxiety is biologically adaptive. Sometimes, though, it is so intense that it interferes with normal functioning. Both **panic disorder** (PD) and **generalised anxiety disorder** (GAD) involve '**free-floating anxiety**', which is accompanied by various physiological and other reactions.
- Classical conditioning might increase PD's severity, but cannot account for its origins. Certain cognitions might act as internal triggers for PD, and the core disturbance in panic might be an abnormality in thinking.
- Stress-induced physiological activity may be interpreted in 'catastrophic' ways, establishing a positive feedback loop between cognitions and bodily activity. However, not everybody reports such cognitions, and it is not obvious why catastrophic thoughts should characterise the disorder.
- PD and GAD have also been addressed by the psychodynamic and medical models. There is evidence for a genetic component in PD. However, if biological factors play a role, it is likely that cognitive factors can modify them.
- It is the irrational nature of the fear involved, together with its interference with normal functioning, that makes a **phobia** a disorder. Three categories of phobias are **agoraphobia**, **social phobia**, and **specific phobias**.
- Wolpe believes that all phobias can be explained in terms of classical conditioning. Their resilience/resistance to extinction

can be explained in terms of both classical and operant conditioning, as in the **two process/factor theory** and the **safety signal hypothesis**.

- Some classes of stimuli can more easily become the objects of phobias than others. This has been explained in terms of **preparedness/prepared conditioning**, although studies claiming to demonstrate preparedness can be explained in terms of non-genetic factors. For example, phobias may be acquired through **observation** and **instruction**. There may be a preparedness for this rather than for direct conditioning.

- In **obsessive–compulsive disorder** (OCD), profound anxiety is reflected in obsessions and compulsions. The four most common obsessional characteristics are **impaired control over mental processes**, **concern of losing control over motor behaviour**, **contamination**, and **checking behaviours**. Compulsions may arise from obsessions. Compulsives recognise their behaviours are senseless, but experience great anxiety if prevented from engaging in them.

- Genetic and learning factors might be involved in OCD. The most promising neurological evidence involves differences between sufferers and non-sufferers in left frontal lobe metabolic activity. However, this might be a consequence or correlate of OCD rather than a cause of it.

- The **anxiety-reduction hypothesis** explains OCD's maintenance but not its origins. The **superstition hypothesis** proposes that the compulsions arise through a chance association between a behaviour and a reinforcer. However, this does not explain the development of intrusive thoughts.

- **Post-traumatic stress disorder** (PTSD) is a response to an extreme psychological/physical experience outside the range of normal human experience. It may occur immediately after the trauma or years later.

- PTSD sufferers all share the experience of a profoundly traumatising event. **Classical conditioning** is involved to the extent that sufferers often show reactions to stimuli present at the time of the trauma. However, not everyone exposed to a traumatic event develops PTSD. This depends on the stressor's nature and severity, individual differences, and the **recovery environment**.

- The return of memories years after a traumatic event suggests that socially valued life roles help people to avoid processing memories of the trauma. However, this prevents such memories being integrated into their world view. As a result, **extinction** of the associated responses cannot occur.

- **Decreased opioid function** may occur in PTSD, and the **locus coeruleus** may act as an 'alarm centre', playing a crucial role in PTSD's genesis. When infused directly into the locus coeruleus, drugs which are effective in treating PTSD also prevent the development of **learned helplessness** in non-humans exposed to inescapable shock.

# EATING DISORDERS

## Introduction and overview

Eating disorders are characterised by physically and/or psychologically harmful eating patterns. In ICD-10, they are categorised as 'behavioural syndromes associated with physiological disturbances and physical factors'. Although there are several types of eating disorder (Brownell & Fairburn, 1995), two broad categories are *anorexia nervosa* and *bulimia nervosa*. This chapter describes the characteristics associated with these disorders and examines explanations of them.

## Anorexia nervosa

Although the characteristics of what is now called anorexia nervosa have been known about for several hundred years (Hartley, 1997), it is only recently that the disorder has attracted much interest. This increased attention is the result of a greater public knowledge of the disorder, and the recent increase in its incidence (although Fombonne, 1995, argues that this increase can be attributed to changes in the diagnostic criteria concerning weight loss: see below).

Anorexia nervosa occurs primarily in females, and female *anorectics* outnumber males by a factor of 15:1 (Hartley, 1997). The disorder usually has its onset in adolescence, the period between 14 and 16 being most common (Hsu, 1990). However, the onset sometimes occurs later in adult life or before adolescence. Lask & Bryant-Waugh (1992), for example, have reported cases of the disorder in children as young as eight. Estimates of anorexia nervosa's incidence vary. American data suggest that one in 250 females may experience the disorder (Lewinsohn *et al.*, 1993). In Britain, the figure is somewhat higher, ranging from one in 100 to four in 100 (Sahakian, 1987), with around 70,000 people recognised as anorectic (Brooke, 1996).

**Box 4.1**   *A typical case of anorexia nervosa*

Frieda had always been a shy, sensitive girl who gave little cause for concern at home or in school. She was bright and did well academically, although she had few friends. In early adolescence, she was somewhat overweight and teased by her family that she would never get a boyfriend unless she lost some weight. She reacted to this by withdrawing and becoming very touchy. Her parents had to be careful about what they said. If offended, Frieda would throw a tantrum and march off to her room.

Frieda began dieting. Initially her family was pleased, but gradually her parents sensed that all was not well. Meal times became battle times. Frieda hardly ate at all. Under pressure, she would take her meals to her room and later, having said that she had eaten everything, her mother would find food hidden away untouched. When her mother caught her deliberately inducing vomiting after a meal, she insisted they go to the family doctor. He found that Frieda had stopped menstruating a few months earlier. Not fooled by the loose, floppy clothes that Frieda was wearing, he insisted on carrying out a full physical examination. Her emaciated body told him as much as he needed to know, and he arranged for Frieda's immediate hospitalisation.

(Adapted from Rosenhan & Seligman, 1984)

As Box 4.1 illustrates, anorexia nervosa is characterised by a prolonged refusal to eat adequate amounts of food which results in deliberate weight loss. As 'Frieda's case' shows, body weight loss is often accompanied by the cessation of menstruation (*amenorrhea*). For a diagnosis of anorexia nervosa to be considered, the individual must weigh less than 85 per cent of normal or expected weight for height, age and sex. As a result of their significant weight loss, anorectics look emaciated. They also show a decline in general health, which is accompanied by many physical problems (Sharp & Freeman, 1993). These include low blood pressure and body temperature, constipation and dehydration. In five to 15 per cent of cases, anorexia nervosa is fatal (Hsu, 1990).

Literally, anorexia nervosa means 'nervous loss of appetite'. However, anorectics are often both hungry and preoccupied with thoughts of food. For example, they may constantly read recipe books and prepare elaborate meals for their friends (Hartley, 1997). Anorectics themselves, however, will avoid most calorie-rich foods, such as meat, milk products, sweets and other desserts, and will often limit their consumption to little more than a lettuce leaf and carrot. They also show reduced pleasure in eating. Although anorectics do not experience deficiencies in taste, they do have a *low hedonic responsiveness* to taste and an aversion to the oral sensation of fat (Sunday & Halmi, 1990).

---

**Box 4.2** *Restricting and binge eating/purging types*

Anorexia nervosa is also characterised by an intense fear of being overweight which does not diminish even when a large amount of weight has been lost. As a consequence of this fear, anorectics take extreme measures to lose weight. In DSM-IV, two sub-types of anorexia nervosa are identified, both of which contribute to the refusal to maintain a body weight above the minimum normal weight. The *restricting type* loses weight through constant fasting and engaging in excessive physical activity. The *binge eating/purging type* alternates between periods of fasting and 'binge eating' (see below) in which normally avoided food is consumed in large quantities. The guilt and shame experienced as a result of the 'binge' lead the anorectic to use laxatives or self-induced vomiting to expel ingested food from the system.

---

One other characteristic of anorexia nervosa is a *distorted body image* in which the individual does not recognise the body's thinness. Even though their appearance may show protruding bones, many anorectics still see themselves as being fat and deny that they are 'wasting away'. As Bruch (1978) has observed, anorectics:

> 'vigorously defend their gruesome emaciation as not being too thin ... they identify with the skeleton-like appearance, actively maintain it and deny its abnormality'.

The fact that many people who would be diagnosed as anorectic do not perceive themselves as having a problem, suggests that data relating to both the incidence and prevalence of the disorder should be treated with caution (Cooper, 1995).

## Explanations of anorexia nervosa

Simmonds (1914) described the case of a girl who was emaciated, had stopped menstruating and showed severe atrophy of the pituitary gland. At the time, and for the next quarter of a century, it was believed that pituitary gland damage caused anorexia nervosa. However, this belief was mistaken and what Simmonds had identified was, in fact, a disorder that actually produces very different symptoms from anorexia nervosa (Colman, 1987). In *Simmonds' disease*, pituitary gland damage is associated with a loss of pubic and underarm hair. This does not happen in anorexia nervosa, and the emaciation Simmonds observed is unusual except in terminal cases. Not surprisingly, therefore, attempts to treat anorexia nervosa with pituitary extracts were unsuccessful.

It has, however, been suggested that anorexia nervosa has a biological basis. Instead of the pituitary gland, it has been proposed that dysfunction in the *hypothalamus* leads to the disorder. Certainly, the hypothalamus plays an important role in the regulation of eating (see Gross & McIlveen, 1998). Kaplan & Woodside (1987) showed that when *noradrenaline* acts on part of the hypothalamus, non-humans begin eating and show a marked preference for carbohydrates. *Serotonin*, by contrast, apparently induces satiation and suppresses appetite, especially for carbohydrates. Any condition which increased serotonin's effects would decrease eating. However, there is not yet sufficient evidence to indicate whether hypothalamic dysfunction and changes in neurotransmitter levels are causes of anorexia nervosa, effects of it or merely correlates (Kaye *et al.*, 1993).

> **Box 4.3** *Corticotrophin-releasing hormone and anorexia nervosa*
>
> Park *et al.* (1995) examined four females with severe restrictive anorexia nervosa who spontaneously volunteered histories of glandular fever-like illnesses immediately preceding their eating disorder's onset. Park *et al.* suggest that viral- or immune-induced alterations in central homeostasis, particularly involving *corticotrophin-releasing hormone*, could trigger and perpetuate a behavioural response leading to a particularly severe form of restrictive anorexia nervosa. This suggestion is speculative, but biologically plausible.

Anorexia nervosa may have a genetic basis. There is a tendency for the disorder to run in families, with first- and second-degree relatives of anorectic individuals being significantly more likely to develop the disorder compared with first- and second-degree relatives of a control group of non-anorectics (Strober & Katz, 1987).

Twin studies have also been used to investigate the role of genetic factors. Askevold & Heiberg (1979) reported a 50 per cent concordance rate for MZs brought up in the same environment, which they see as strong evidence that genes play an important role. However, in the absence of concordance rates for DZs and MZs reared apart, this claim is difficult to evaluate. Holland *et al.* (1984) reported a concordance rate of 55 per cent for MZs brought up in the same environment and seven per cent for DZs. Although this difference hints at genetic involvement, the concordance rate suggests that if genes do play a role, it is likely to be a small one (Treasure & Holland, 1991).

> **Box 4.4** *Anorexia and the anterior temporal lobes*
>
> According to Lask (cited in Kennedy, 1997), a blood flow deficiency in the anterior temporal lobes, which interpret vision, explains why anorectics see themselves as fat when they are thin. However, people with the deficiency would need other triggers to develop the disorder. These might include stress, a perfectionist personality and a society that promoted thinness (see text).

Other theories of anorexia nervosa are more social and psychological in their orientation. The psychodynamic model proposes that the disorder represents an unconscious effort by a girl to remain pre-pubescent. As a result of overdependence on the parents, some girls might fear becoming sexually mature and independent. As noted earlier, anorexia nervosa is associated with amenorrhea, and psychodynamic theorists see this as enabling the anorectic to circumvent growing up and achieving adult responsibilities. Certainly, to achieve puberty, we must attain a particular level of body fat, and evidence suggests that anorectics will eat, provided they do not gain weight.

An alternative psychodynamic account proposes that the disorder may allow a girl to avoid the issue of her sexuality. The weight loss that occurs prevents the rounding of the breasts and hips, and the body takes on a 'boy-like' appearance. This might be a way of avoiding the issue of sexuality in general, and the prospect of pregnancy in particular.

Yet another psychodynamic account sees the disorder as attempts by adolescents to *separate* themselves from their parents and establish their own identities. Psychodynamic theorists argue that the parents of anorectics tend to be domineering, and that the disorder reflects an attempt to exert individuality. Many female anorectics are 'good girls', who do well in school and are cooperative and well-behaved (Bemis, 1978). Bemis argues that this leads them to feel they have no choices and are being controlled by the desires and demands of others. One way of exerting individuality is to assume control over what is most concretely one's self – the body. Thinness and starvation, then, are signs of self-control and independence.

Although there may be some truth in psychodynamic accounts of anorexia nervosa, at least two observations challenge them. First, some seem to apply only to females. It is impossible to see how avoiding the prospect of pregnancy could apply to male anorectics. Second, all of the accounts have difficulty in explaining anorexia nervosa's occurrence after adolescence.

**Figure 4.1** *The much publicised English anorectic twins, Samantha and Michaela Kendall. Despite receiving treatment in the USA, Samantha eventually died. Michaela died three years later.*

The behavioural model sees anorexia nervosa as a *phobia* (see Chapter 3) concerning the possibility of gaining weight. Indeed, anorexia nervosa might be more appropriately called *weight phobia* (Crisp, 1967). The phobia is assumed to be the result of the impact of social norms, values and roles. Garner *et al.* (1980) have claimed that the winners of Miss America and the centrefolds in *Playboy* magazine have consistently been below the average female weight and have become significantly more so since 1959. Thus, the *cultural idealisation* of the slender female (as represented by 'supermodels') may be one cause of the fear of being fat (Petkova, 1997). The pressures have become so great that, in America at least, normal eating for women is characterised by dieting! (Polivy & Herman, 1985).

In at least some occupations, such as ballet dancing and modelling, there is considerable pressure on women to be thin and the incidence of anorexia nervosa in these occupations is higher than in the population in general (Garfinkel & Garner, 1982). However, not all ballet dancers, models and so on, who diet to be slim develop eating disorders (Cooper, 1995). For Wooley & Wooley (1983):

'an increasingly stringent cultural standard of thinness for women has been accompanied by a steadily increasing incidence of serious eating disorders in women'.

Support for the claim that societal norms can be influential in this respect comes from evidence about eating disorders in other cultures. In at least some non-Western cultures (including China, Singapore and Malaysia), the incidence of anorexia nervosa is much lower than in Western societies (Lee *et al.*, 1992). Additionally, cases of anorexia nervosa reported in black populations of Western and non-Western cultures are significantly lower than those in white populations (Sui-Wah, 1989).

---

**Box 4.5** *Sindy and anorexia nervosa*

According to Hill (cited in Uhlig, 1996), women's fashion magazines play a part in shaping young girls' perceptions of desirable figures, but are not as influential as classmates, mothers and toys. According to Hill:

'[Sindy] is now unashamedly blonde, pointedly thin, [and] dressed immaculately ... Not only does 90s Sindy depict the ideal appearance and lifestyle of 90s women, she does so for girls only halfway to puberty'.

One consequence of young children's preoccupation with weight and shape is osteoporosis ('brittle bone' disease) more usually

---

> associated with elderly women (Hall, 1997). Some companies have
> withdrawn their advertising campaigns from magazines which feature 'skeletal' models on the grounds that it is 'irresponsible ... to
> have models of anorexic proportions' (Weaver, 1996).

One puzzling observation which is difficult for theories to account for is the development of anorexia nervosa in people unable to see. As noted earlier (see page 67), body image disturbance is one of the 'hallmarks' of anorexia nervosa. However, Yager *et al.* (1986) describe the case of a 28-year-old woman, blind from age two, who had become anoretic at age 21. Touyz *et al.* (1988) report a case of anorexia nervosa in a woman blind from birth. Although neither research team offered a satisfactory explanation for their findings, both agreed that blindness either from birth or a very early age does not preclude anorexia nervosa's development, and that people do not have to be actually able to see themselves to desire a slimmer physique (see also Box 4.4).

**Figure 4.2**    *Kate Moss (left), well-known supermodel, and two models from Yes! magazine (right), demonstrating that physical beauty or ideal body shape/size can be defined in more than one way, within the same culture and at the same point in time*

# Bulimia nervosa

Literally, bulimia comes from the Greek *bous* meaning 'ox' and *limos* meaning 'hunger'. The disorder was first extensively investigated by Russell (1979), who saw it as 'an ominous variant' of anorexia nervosa. Bulimia nervosa is characterised by periodic episodes of 'compulsive' or 'binge' eating, the rapid and seemingly uncontrolled consumption of food, especially that rich in carbohydrates.

The binge is terminated either by abdominal pain or, in the case of the *purging type*, by the expulsion of food using diuretics, laxatives or self-induced vomiting. Some bulimics begin their binges by eating coloured 'marker' foods and, after they have finished, will continue purging until the marker has re-emerged (Colman, 1987). A typical binge might include the consumption of a large amount of ice cream, packets of crisps, a pizza and several cans of fizzy drink. As well as their high calorific content, most foods consumed by bulimics have textures that aid rapid consumption. Thus, food tends to be 'wolfed down' rather than chewed properly. With the *non-purging type*, strict dieting or vigorous exercise (rather than regular purging) occurs.

'Binge eating' itself is actually quite common and many people admit to indulging occasionally (Polivy & Herman, 1985). In bulimia nervosa, however, the *frequency* of such behaviour is much higher, averaging at least two or three times a week, and sometimes as often as 30 times a week.

---

**Box 4.6** *A typical case of bulimia nervosa*

Miss A. was a 22-year-old single clerk, who was referred by her doctor for treatment of 'psychiatric problems'. She had a three-year history of uncontrolled overeating. Although she was not originally obese, she disliked her 'square face' and developed a sensitive personality. After failing an examination and being unable to study in further education, she started to relieve her boredom and comfort

---

herself by overeating. Her binges occurred four times per week and lasted one to three hours each.

Triggers included feelings of emptiness and critical remarks from others. On average, she secretly consumed 800 g of bread and biscuits. Such episodes were followed by abdominal bloating, guilt and dysphoria (inappropriate emotional feelings). There was nausea, but no vomiting. She took excessive laxatives (usually prune juice) to purge and 'calm' herself, restricted food intake and exercised excessively in the next one to two days. Her body weight fluctuated by up to 4 kg per week, but her menstrual cycle was normal.

Examination revealed a girl who was fully conscious of what she was doing and who felt helpless over the 'attacks of overeating'. She desired a body weight of 45 kg and disparaged her waistline and square face, which made her 'look like a pig'. She found food dominated her life, and likened her problem to heroin addiction. There was a persistent request for laxatives.

(Adapted from Lee et al., 1992)

Most bulimics are women, with fewer than five per cent of cases presenting for treatment being men (Cooper, 1995). The disorder usually begins in adolescence or early adulthood and generally appears later than in anorexia nervosa. Bulimia nervosa is also more frequent than anorexia nervosa and may affect as many as five per cent of the population. Like anorectics, bulimics have what ICD-10 calls 'an intrusive fear of fatness', and they are unduly concerned with their body weight and shape (hence they take the drastic steps described above to control their weight). Cutts & Barrios (1986), for example, asked bulimics to imagine gaining weight. Physiological measures indicated increased heart rate and muscle tension compared with non-bulimic controls performing the same task.

Whilst the discrepancy between actual body weight and desired body weight is generally no greater than among non-bulimics, the discrepancy between *estimations* of body size and desired size is substantial (Cooper, 1995). Although bulimics are mostly able to maintain a normal body weight, they tend to fluctuate between weight gain and weight loss. The binge–purge behaviour is typically accompanied by guilty feelings. The purging of food produces feelings of relief and a commitment to a severely restrictive diet which ultimately fails (Sue *et al.*, 1994).

Clearly, bulimics recognise their eating behaviour is abnormal and feel frustrated by it. However, they are unable to control the behaviour voluntarily. Because of the guilty feelings, bingeing and purging are usually carried out in secret and, consequently, many bulimics go unrecognised even to close friends and family. Moreover, because there is not a constant weight loss, and because the bulimic's eating habits may appear normal in public, the estimate given for the number of cases must be treated cautiously.

Purging does, however, produce some effects that might be noticeable to others. One of these is a 'puffy' facial appearance (a consequence of swollen parotid glands caused by vomiting). Another is a deterioration in tooth enamel (caused by the stomach acid produced when vomiting occurs). A third is the development of calluses over the back of the hand (caused by rubbing the hand against the upper teeth when the fingers are pushed into the throat to induce vomiting). Other associated physiological effects include digestive tract damage, dehydration and nutritional imbalances. Psychological effects include anxiety, sleep disturbances and depression (see below).

Associations between *self-mutilative behaviour* and bulimia nervosa have also been reported. Parry-Jones & Parry-Jones (1993) examined 25 bulimic cases reported from the late seventeenth to the late nineteenth centuries. They found four instances of self-mutilative behaviour and argue that such historical evidence offers some support for the suggested connection between eating disorders and self-mutilation.

**Box 4.7**   *Blood-letting and bulimia*

An unusual form of self-mutilation was reported by Parkin & Eagles (1993) who studied three cases of *blood-letting* in association with bulimia nervosa. All three had some medical training and began blood-letting after they had acquired sufficient expertise in the insertion of intravenous cannulae and the necessary implements. Each bulimic appeared to derive similar psychological benefit from the blood-letting which seemed to serve much the same function as bingeing and vomiting in that it relieved feelings of anxiety, tension and anger.

## Explanations of bulimia nervosa

As with anorexia nervosa, there are several theoretical approaches to understanding the cause of bulimia nervosa. As mentioned previously (see page 68), certain neurotransmitters have been implicated in the regulation of eating behaviour. Neurotransmitters may also be implicated in bulimia nervosa. For example, abnormal neurotransmitter activity might account for the periodic carbohydrate bingeing.

*Hormones* and *endorphins* may also play a mediating role. Lydiard *et al.* (1993) reported that levels of *cholecystokinin octapeptide* (CCK-8) were significantly lower in 11 drug-free female bulimics than 16 age-matched controls. Since there was no correlation between the mean frequency of binge eating or vomiting and scores on the *Eating Disorders Inventory*, the bulimics' unusual eating habits do not seem to be responsible for the decreased levels of CCK-8.

Other research has found that *plasma endorphins* are elevated in people with bulimia nervosa (and, interestingly, in those who self-mutilate: cf. Parkin & Eagles', 1993, study described in Box 4.7). However, whether the elevated levels are a cause or a result of bulimia nervosa remains to be established. Additionally, the genetic evidence for bulimia nervosa is much weaker than that for anorexia nervosa. Kendler *et al.* (1991), for example, have reported a concordance rate of only 23 per cent for MZs and nine per cent for DZs (see page 69).

---

**Box 4.8**  *The disinhibition hypothesis*

One psychological approach to understanding bulimia nervosa is Ruderman's (1986) *disinhibition hypothesis*. This distinguishes between 'unrestrained' and 'restrained' eaters, the latter being people who constantly monitor their weight and constantly diet. Sometimes, 'restrained' eaters believe they have overeaten, a belief that may be accompanied by the thought that, since the diet has been broken, there is no reason why more should not be eaten. This *disinhibition* leads to the consumption of more food, which is followed by purging in an attempt to reduce the weight gained by the binge eating. As well as breaking a diet, other *disinhibiting factors* include alcohol. For Ruderman, the food intake pattern of highly weight-conscious people is characterised by an all-or-nothing rigidity which makes them susceptible to binge eating.

---

Because anorexia nervosa and bulimia nervosa share many characteristics, some researchers believe they can be explained in the same way. Garner (1986) has argued that it is seriously misleading to consider the disorders as being psychologically dissimilar. Echoing Garner, Bee (1992) describes them as 'variations on a basic theme' rather than distinctly different disorders. Garner has shown that as well as sharing many psychological traits (such as perfectionism), anorectics and bulimics also share the same goal of maintaining a sub-optimal body weight. Moreover, a particular individual may often move *between* the two disorders in the quest for thinness.

According to Waller (1993), sexual abuse is related to eating disorders, particularly those involving bulimic features. In a study of 100 women with eating disorders, Waller found that *borderline personality disorder* explains at least a small part of the link between sexual abuse and bulimic behaviour, especially as regards the frequency of bingeing. This alleged link has, however, been challenged (Cooper, 1995). Even if it exists, other factors are surely involved. For example, people with eating disorders often have a personal history of affective disorder (particularly depression: see Chapter 2). Piran *et al.* (1985) found that among 18 patients with a lifetime history of major depression, the depressive symptoms preceded the eating disorder's onset by at least one year in eight cases, post-dated its onset in six, and occurred around the same time in the other four. Also, binge eating, mood and purging vary seasonally with bulimia nervosa. This might suggest that a vulnerability to depression (or seasonal affective disorder: see Chapter 2) increases the predisposition to eating disorders, and an episode of depression might contribute to either the initation of its symptoms or its maintenance (Cooper, 1995).

## Conclusions

Several theories of anorexia nervosa and bulimia nervosa have been proposed. Although some are more plausible than others, and have more supporting evidence, no theory yet has explanatory power over all others. Possibly, the two eating disorders do not have single discrete causes, and there may be complex chains of events which interact to precipitate them.

## Summary

- **Anorexia nervosa** occurs more frequently in females than males and usually appears in adolescence. It is characterised by a prolonged refusal to eat adequate amounts of food, resulting in deliberate weight loss. To be diagnosed as anorectic, an individual must weigh less than 85 per cent of normal/expected weight for height, age and sex. In five to 15 per cent of cases, anorexia is fatal.

- Because of their fear of being overweight, anorectics take extreme measures to lose weight. The **restricting type** engages in constant fasting/excessive physical activity, whilst the **binge eating/purging type** alternates between periods of fasting and 'binge eating', food being expelled by laxatives or self-induced vomiting.

- Damage to the **hypothalamus** might cause anorexia nervosa. In non-humans, stimulation of the hypothalamus by **noradrenaline** produces eating and a preference for carbohydrates. **Serotonin** produces the opposite effect. **Corticotrophin-releasing hormone** and **anterior temporal lobe** deficiencies have also been implicated. However, whether brain dysfunction and/or changes in neurotransmitters are causes, effects or correlates is unclear. If **genetic** factors are involved, their role is likely to be small.

- There are several **psychodynamic** accounts of anorexia nervosa. Whilst some observations are consistent with them, they apply only to females and focus on anorexia exclusively as an adolescent disorder.

- The **behavioural** model sees anorexia as a **phobia** of gaining weight, resulting from the impact of social norms, values and roles. The current cultural idealisation of the 'slender female' may be one cause of the fear of being fat. A lower incidence of anorexia in other cultures supports this perspective.

- One difficulty for all theories is in explaining anorexia's development in people blind from birth. This finding makes the importance of a distorted body image as one of the disorder's characteristics difficult to explain.

- Most **bulimics** are women, and **bulimia nervosa** usually begins in adolescence or early adulthood. The **purging type** is characterised by frequent episodes of compulsive/binge eating, ended either by abdominal pain or the use of diuretics, laxatives, and/or self-induced vomiting. The **non-purging type** counteracts the food intake either by strict dieting or vigorous exercise.

- Like anorectics, bulimics are unduly concerned with their body weight/shape. Although able to maintain a normal body weight, they tend to fluctuate between gain and loss. Bulimics recognise the abnormal nature of their eating behaviour, but are unable to control it. Bulimia is also associated with **self-mutilative behaviour**, one unusual form being **blood-letting**.

- **Noradrenaline**, **serotonin**, **hormones** and **endorphins** may all play mediating roles in bulimia nervosa. For example, elevated **plasma endorphin** levels have been found in bulimics, although whether these are a cause, consequence or correlate of the disorder is not known.

- The **disinhibition hypothesis** proposes that when 'restrained eaters' believe they have overeaten, their eating becomes 'disinhibited'. This is followed by purging to reduce the weight gained. Highly weight-conscious people display all-or-nothing rigidity, making them susceptible to binge eating.

- Anorexia and bulimia may be distinct disorders or 'variations on a theme'. Anorectics and bulimics share many psychological traits, along with the goal of maintaining a sub-optimal body weight. The same person may also alternate between the two disorders.

- Sexual abuse is correlated with some eating disorders, and **borderline personality disorder** partly links the two. However, seasonal affective disorder may increase a predisposition to eating disorders. A depressive episode might contribute to the initiation of an eating disorder or its maintenance.

ABRAHAM, K. (1911) Notes on the psychoanalytical investigation and treatment of manic-depressive insanity and allied conditions. Originally written in 1911 and later published in E. Jones (Ed.) *Selected Papers of Karl Abraham, MD*. London: The Hogarth Press.

ABRAMSON, L.Y., SELIGMAN, M.E.P. & TEASDALE, J.D. (1978) Learned helplessness in humans: Critique and reformulation. *Journal of Abnormal Psychology, 87, 49–74*.

ALLEN, M. (1976) Twin studies of affective illness. *Archives of General Psychiatry, 33, 1476–1478*.

ASKEVOLD, F. & HEIBERG, A. (1979) Anorexia nervosa: Two cases in discordant MZ twins. *Psychological Monographs, 70, 1–70*.

BALON, R., JORDAN, M., PHOL, R. & YERAGNI, V. (1989) Family history of anxiety disorders in control subjects with lactate-induced panic attacks. *American Journal of Psychiatry, 146, 1304–1306*.

BARON, M., RISCH, N., HAMBURGER, R., MANDEL, B., KUSHNER, S., NEWMAN, M., DRUMER, D. & BELMAKER, R. (1987) Genetic linkage between X-chromosome markers and bipolar affective illness. *Nature, 326, 289–292*.

BARR, C.E., MEDNICK, S.A. & MUNK-JORGENSON, P. (1990) Exposure to influenza epidemics during gestation and adult schizophrenia: A forty-year study. *Archives of General Psychiatry, 47, 869–874*.

BATESON, G., JACKSON, D., HALEY, J. & WEAKLAND, J. (1956) Toward a theory of schizophrenia. *Behavioural Science, 1, 251–264*.

BECK, A.T. (1974) The development of depression: A cognitive model. In R.J. Friedman & M.M. Katz (Eds) *The Psychology of Depression: Contemporary Theory and Research*. New York: Wiley.

BECK, A.T. & YOUNG, J.E. (1978) College blues. *Psychology Today*, September, 80–92.

BEE, H. (1992) *The Developing Child* (7th edition). New York: HarperCollins.

BELFER, P.L. & GLASS, C.R. (1992) Agoraphobic anxiety and fear of fear: Test of a cognitive–attentional model. *Journal of Anxiety Disorders, 6, 133–146*.

BEMIS, K.M. (1978) Current approaches to the aetiology and treatment of anorexia nervosa. *Psychological Bulletin, 85, 593–617*.

BENDER, M. (1995) The war goes on. *The Psychologist, 8, 78–79*.

BENNETT, W. (1997) Daughter dead after living like a monk in a room for 14 years. *The Daily Telegraph*, 5 September, 3.

BENTALL, R. (1996) The illness that defies diagnosis. *The Times*, 20 May, 14.

BICK, P.A. & KINSBOURNE, M. (1987) Auditory hallucinations and subvocal speech in schizophrenic patients. *American Journal of Psychiatry, 32, 297–306*.

BLEULER, E. (1911) *Dementia Praecox or the Group of Schizophrenias*. New York: International University Press.

BLEULER, M.E. (1978) The long-term course of schizophrenic psychoses. In L.C. Wynne, R.L. Cromwell & S. Mathyse (Eds) *The Nature of Schizophrenia: New Approaches to Research and Treatment*. New York: Wiley.

BRACHA, H.S., TORREY, E.F., BIGELOW, L.B., LOHR, J.B. & LININGTON, B.B. (1991) Subtle signs of prenatal maldevelopment of the head ectoderm in schizophrenia: A preliminary monozygotic twin study. *Biological Psychiatry, 30, 719–725*.

BROOKE, S. (1996) The anorexic man. *The Sunday Times* (Style Section), 11 February, 17.

BROWN, G.W. & HARRIS, T.O. (1978) *Social Origins of Depression: A Study of Psychiatric Disorder in Women*. London: Tavistock.

BROWNELL, K.D. & FAIRBURN, C.G. (1995) *Eating Disorders and Obesity: A Comprehensive Handbook*. New York: Guildford.

BRUCH, H. (1978) *Eating Disorders: Obesity, Anorexia Nervosa and the Person Within*. New York: Basic Books.

BUNNEY, W., GOODWIN, F. & MURPHY, D. (1972) The 'switch process' in manic-depressive illness. *Archives of General Psychiatry*, 27, 312–317.

CALLAGHAN, P. & O'CARROLL, M. (1993) Making women mad. *Nursing Times*, 89, 26–29.

CARSON, R. (1989) Personality. *Annual Review of Psychology*, 40, 227–248.

CHUA, S.E. & McKENNA, P.J. (1995) Schizophrenia – a brain disease? A critical review of structural and functional cerebral abnormality in the disorder. *British Journal of Psychiatry*, 166, 563–582.

CLARIDGE, G. (1987) The continuum of psychosis and the gene. *British Journal of Psychiatry*, 150, 129–133 (correspondence).

CLARK, D.M. (1993) Treating panic attacks. *The Psychologist*, 6, 73–74.

COCHRANE, R. (1983) *The Social Creation of Mental Illness*. London: Longman.

COCHRANE, R. (1995) Women and depression. *Psychology Review*, 2, 20–24.

COLMAN, A.M. (1987) *Facts, Fallacies and Frauds in Psychology*. London: Unwin Hyman.

COMINGS, D.E. & COMINGS, B.G. (1987) Hereditary agoraphobia and obsessive-compulsive behaviour in relatives of patients with Gilles de la Tourette's syndrome. *British Journal of Psychiatry*, 151, 195–199.

COOPER, P.J. (1995) Eating disorders. In A.A. Lazarus & A.M. Colman (Eds) *Abnormal Psychology*. London: Longman.

CRISP, A.H. (1967) Anorexia nervosa. *Hospital Medicine*, 1, 713–718.

CROOK, T. & ELIOT, J. (1980) Parental death during childhood and adult depression: A critical review of the literature. *Psychological Bulletin*, 87, 252–259.

CROW, T.J. & DONE, D.J. (1992) Prenatal exposure to influenza does not cause schizophrenia. *British Journal of Psychiatry*, 161, 390–393.

CROW, T.J., CROSS, A.G., JOHNSTONE, E.C. & OWEN, F. (1982) Two syndromes in schizophrenia and their pathogenesis. In F.A. Henn & G.A. Nasrallah (Eds) *Schizophrenia as a Brain Disease*. New York: Oxford University Press.

CUTTS, T.F. & BARRIOS, B.A. (1986) Fear of weight gain among bulimic and non-disturbed females. *Behaviour Therapy*, 17, 626–636.

DAVIDSON, R.J. (1992) Anterior cerebral asymmetry and the nature of emotion. *Brain and Cognition*, 20, 280–299.

DAVIS, J.M. (1974) A two-factor theory of schizophrenia. *Journal of Psychiatric Research*, 11, 25–30.

DAVIS, K.L., KAHN, R.S., KO, G. & DAVIDSON, M. (1991). Dopamine in schizophrenia; a review and reconceptualization. *American Journal of Psychiatry*, 148, 1474–1486.

DAVISON, G & NEALE, J. (1990) *Abnormal Psychology* (5th Edition). New York: Wiley.

DILSAVER, J. (1989) Panic disorder. *American Family Physician*, 39, 167–173.

DIXON, P., REHLING, G. & SHIWACH, R. (1993) Peripheral victims of the Herald of Free Enterprise disaster. *British Journal of Medical Psychology*, 66, 193–202.

DOANE, J.A., FALLOON, I.R.H., GOLDSTEIN, M.J. & MINTZ, J. (1985) Parental affective style and the treatment of schizophrenia: Predicting course of illness and social functioning. *Archives of General Psychiatry*, 42, 34–42.

EGELAND, J., GERHARD, D., PAULS, D., SUSSEX, J., KIDD, K., ALLEN, C., HOSTETTER, A. & HOUSEMAN, D. (1987) Bipolar affective disorder linked to DNA markers on chromosome 11. *Nature*, 325, 783–787.

EYSENCK, H.J. (1967) *The Biological Basis of Personality*. Springfield, ILL: Charles C. Thomas.

FERSTER, C. (1965) Classification of behaviour pathology. In L. Krasner & L. Ullman (Eds) *Research in Behaviour Modification*. New York: Holt, Rinehart & Winston.

FIELDS, H. (1991) Depression and pain: A neurobiological model. Neuropsychiatry, *Neuropsychology and Behavioural Neurology*, 4, 83–92.

FOMBONNE, E. (1995) Anorexia nervosa: No evidence of an increase. *British Journal of Psychiatry*, 166, 462–471.

FREUD, S. (1909) *Analysis of a Phobia in a Five-Year-Old Boy*. London: The Hogarth Press.

FREUD, S. (1917) *Mourning and Melancholia*. London: The Hogarth Press.

FROMM-REICHMAN, F. (1948) Notes on the development of treatment of schizophrenics by psychoanalytic psychotherapy. *Psychiatry*, 11, 263–273.

FRUDE, N. (1998) *Understanding Abnormal Psychology*. Oxford: Blackwell.

GARFINKEL, P.E. & GARNER, D.M. (1982) *Anorexia Nervosa: A Multidimensional Perspective*. New York: Basic Books.

GARNER, D.M. (1986) Cognitive–behavioural therapy for eating disorders. *The Clinical Psychologist*, 39, 36–39.

GARNER, D.M., GARFINKEL, P.E., SCHWARZ, D. & THOMPSON, M. (1980) Cultural expectations of thinness in women. *Psychological Reports*, 47, 483–491.

GELDER, M., GATH, D. & MAYON, R. (1989) *The Oxford Textbook of Psychiatry* (2nd edition). Oxford: Oxford University Press.

GEORGE, M.S. & BALLENGER, J.C. (1992) The neuropsychology of panic disorder: The emerging role of the right parahippocampal region. *Journal of Anxiety Disorders*, 6, 181–188.

GOLDSTEIN, M. & PALMER, J. (1975) *The Experience of Anxiety: A Casebook* (2nd edition). New York: Oxford University Press.

GORMAN, C. (1997) Anatomy of melancholy. *Time*, 12 May, 30.

GOTLIB, I.A. & COLBY, C.A. (1995) *Psychological Aspects of Depression: Towards a Cognitive-Interpersonal Integration*. Chichester: Wiley.

GOTTESMAN, I. (1991) *Schizophrenia Genesis*. New York: W.H. Freeman.

GOTTESMAN, I.I. & SHIELDS, J. (1972) *Schizophrenia and Genetics: A Twin Study Vantage Point*. New York: Academic Press.

GREEN, B.L. (1994) Psychosocial research in traumatic stress: An update. *Journal of Traumatic Stress*, 7, 341–363.

GROSS, R. & MCILVEEN, R. (1998) *Psychology: A New Introduction*. London: Hodder & Stoughton

HAAGA, D.A. & BECK, A.T. (1992) Cognitive therapy. In S. Pakyel (Ed.) *Handbook of Affective Disorders* (2nd edition). Cambridge: Cambridge University Press.

HALL, C. (1997) Mothers starve 'fat' babies. *The Daily Telegraph*, 16 April, 9.

HAMMEN, C.L. (1985) Predicting depression: A cognitive-behavioural perspective. In P. Kendall (Ed.) *Advances in Cognitive-Behavioural Research and Therapy*, Volume 4. New York: Academic Press.

HARRISON, P. (1995) Schizophrenia: A misunderstood disease. *Psychology Review*, 2, 2–6.

HARTLEY, P. (1997) Eating disorders: myths and misconceptions. *Biological Sciences Review*, 9, 25–27.

HESTON, L.L. (1966) Psychiatric disorders in foster-home-reared children of schizophrenic mothers. *British Journal of Psychiatry*, 122, 819–825.

HESTON, L.L. (1970) The genetics of schizophrenia and schizoid disease. *Science*, 167, 249–256.

HIGHFIELD, R. (1995) Revealed: the source of those voices we hear. *The Daily Telegraph*, 28 June, 18.

HIGHFIELD, R. (1996) Don't worry, it's just in your genes. *The Daily Telegraph*, 20 November, 5.

HIGHFIELD, R. (1997a) Faulty gene linked to schizophrenia. *The Daily Telegraph*, 22 January, 11.

HIGHFIELD, R. (1997b) Depression in women due to 'chemistry'. *The Daily Telegraph*, 13 May, 5.

HODGSON, R.J. & RACHMAN, S. (1972) The effects of contamination and washing in obsessional patients. *Behaviour Research and Therapy*, 10, 111–117.

HOLLAND, A.J., HALL, A., MURRAY, R., RUSSELL, G.F.M. & CRISP, A.H. (1984) Anorexia nervosa: A study of 34 twin pairs and one set of triplets. *British Journal of Psychiatry*, 145, 414–418.

HSU, L.K. (1990) *Eating Disorders*. New York: Guilford.

HUGDAHL, K. & ÖHMAN, A. (1977) Effects of instruction on acquisition of electrodermal response to fear relevant stimuli. *Journal of Experimental Psychology*, 3, 608–618.

HUNT, L. (1995) Why a fear of spiders is all in the genes. *The Independent*, 20 December, 17.

HUNT, N. (1997) Trauma of war. *The Psychologist*, 10, 357–360.

IVERSEN, L.L. (1979) The chemistry of the brain. *Scientific American*, 241, 134–149.

JAMISON, K. (1989) Mood disorders and patterns of creativity in British writers and artists. *Psychiatry*, 52, 125–134.

JOHNSON, D. (1989) Schizophrenia as a brain disease. *American Psychologist*, 44, 553–555.

JOHNSTON, R. (1997) This is not my beautiful wife … *New Scientist*, 22 March, 19.

JOSEPH, S., YULE, W., WILLIAMS, R. & HODGKSINSON, P. (1993) Increased substance use in survivors of the Herald of Free Enterprise. *British Journal of Medical Psychology*, 66, 185–192.

KAPLAN, A. & WOODSIDE, D. (1987) Biological aspects of anorexia nervosa and bulimia nervosa. *Journal of Consulting and Clinical Psychology*, 55, 645–653.

KAY, R.W. (1994) Geomagnetic storms: Association with incidence of depression as measured by hospital admission. *British Journal of Psychiatry*, 164, 403–409.

KAYE, W.H., WELTZIN, T.E. & HSU, L.G. (1993) Relationship between anorexia nervosa and obsessive and compulsive behaviours. *Psychiatric Annals*, 23, 365–373.

KELSOE, J.R., GINNS, E.I., EGELAND, J.A. & GERHARD, D.S. (1989) Re-evaluation of the linkage relationship between chromosome 11 loci and the gene for bipolar disorder in the Old Order Amish. *Nature*, 342, 238–243.

KENDLER, K.S., McLEAN, C., NEALE, M., KESSLER, R., HEATH, A. & EAVES, L. (1991) The genetic epidemiology of bulimia nervosa. *American Journal of Psychiatry*, 148, 1627–1637.

KENNEDY, D. (1997) Anorexia is linked to brain deficiency. *The Times*, 14 April, 5.

KETY, S.S. (1975) Biochemistry of the major psychoses. In A. Freedman, H. Kaplan & B. Sadock (Eds) *Comprehensive Textbook of Psychiatry*. Baltimore: Williams & Wilkins.

KETY, S.S., ROSENTHAL, D., WENDER, P.H. & SCHULSINGER, F. (1968) The types and prevalence of mental illness in the biological and adoptive families of adopted schizophrenics. In D. Rosenthal & S.S. Kety (Eds) *The Transmission of Schizophrenia*. Elmsford, NY: Pergamon Press.

KIMBLE, D.P. (1988) *Biological Psychology*. New York: Holt, Rinehart & Winston.

KLANING, U., MORTENSEN, P.B. & KYVIK, K.D. (1996) Increased occurrence of schizophrenia and other psychiatric illnesses among twins. *British Journal of Psychiatry*, 168, 688–692.

KLEBANOFF, L.D. (1959) A comparison of parental attitudes of mothers of schizophrenics, brain injured and normal children. *American Journal of Psychiatry*, 24, 445–454.

KOLB, L.C. (1987) A neuropsychological hypothesis explaining post-traumatic stress disorders. *American Journal of Psychiatry*, 144, 989–995.

KRAEPELIN, E. (1913) *Clinical Psychiatry: A Textbook for Physicians* (translated by A. Diffendorf). New York: Macmillan.

KRYSTAL, J.H., KOSTEN, T.R. & SOUTHWICK, S. (1989) *Neurobiological aspects of PTSD*: A review of clinical and preclinical studies. Behaviour Therapy, 20, 177–198.

LASK, B. & BRYANT-WAUGH, R. (1992) Childhood onset of anorexia nervosa and related eating disorders. *Journal of Child Psychology and Psychiatry, 3*, 281–300.

LAUGHLIN, H.P. (1967) *The Neuroses*. Washington, DC: Butterworth.

LEE, S., HSU, L.K.G. & WING, Y.K. (1992) Bulimia nervosa in Hong Kong Chinese patients. *British Journal of Psychiatry*, 161, 545–551.

LEMONICK, M.D. (1997) The Mood Molecule. *Time*, September 29, 67–73.

LEON, G.R. (1990) *Case Histories of Psychopathology*. Boston: Allyn & Bacon.

LEWINSOHN, P.M. (1974) A behavioural approach to depression. In R. Friedman & M. Katz (Eds) *The Psychology of Depression: Contemporary Theory and Research*. Washington, DC: Winston/Wiley.

LEWINSOHN, P.M. & HOBERMAN, H.M. (1982) Depression. In A.S. Bellack, M. Hersen & A.E. Kazdin (Eds) *International Handbook of Behaviour Modification and Therapy*. New York: Plenum.

LEWINSOHN, P.M., HOPS, H. & ROBERTS, R.E. (1993) Adolescent psychopathology: I. Prevalence and incidence of depression and other DSM-3-R disorders in high school students. *Journal of Abnormal Psychology*, 102, 133–144.

LIDZ, T. (1973) Commentary on 'A critical review of recent adoption, twin and family studies of schizophrenia: Behavioural genetics perspectives'. *Schizophrenia Bulletin*, 2, 402–412.

LYDIARD, R.B., BREWERTON, T.D., FOSSEY, M.D., LARAIA, M.T., STUART, G., BEINFIELD, M.C. & BALLENGER, J.C. (1993) CSF cholecystokinin octapeptide in patients with bulimia nervosa and in comparison with normal subjects. *American Journal of Psychiatry*, 150, 1099–1101.

MacPHILLAMY, D. & LEWINSOHN, P.M. (1974) Depression as a function of levels of desired and obtained pleasure. *Journal of Abnormal Psychology*, 83, 651–657.

MAHER, B. (1968) The shattered language of schizophrenia. *Psychology Today*, 30ff.

McGUIRE, P.K., BENCH, C.J., FRITH, C.D., MARKS, I.M., FRACKOWIAK, R.S.J. & DOLAN, R.J. (1994) Functional asymmetry of obsessive–compulsive phenomena. *British Journal of Psychiatry*, 164, 459–468.

MEDNICK, S. (1958) A learning theory approach to schizophrenia. *Psychological Bulletin*, 55, 316–327.

MENNINGER, W.W. (Ed.) (1995) *Fear of Humiliation – Integrated Treatment of Social Phobia and Comorbid Conditions*. New Jersey: Jason Aronson.

MILLER, W.R., ROSELLINI, R.A. & SELIGMAN, M.E.P. (1977) Learned helplessness and depression. In J.D. Maser & M.E.P. Seligman (Eds) *Psychopathology: Experimental Models*. San Francisco: W.H. Freeman.

MOWRER, O.H. (1947) On the dual nature of learning – a reinterpretation of 'conditioning' and 'problem-solving'. *Harvard Educational Review*, 17, 102–148.

MURRAY, E.J. & FOOTE, F. (1979) The origins of fear of snakes. *Behaviour Research and Therapy*, 17, 489–493.

MURRAY, I. (1997) Popeye phobia was no laughing matter. *The Times*, 4 August, 3.

MURRAY, J. (1995) *Prevention of Anxiety and Depression in Vulnerable Groups*. London: Gaskell.

MURRAY, R., OON, M., RODNIGHT, R., BIRLEY, J. & SMITH, A. (1979) Increased excretion of dimethyltryptamine and certain features of psychosis. *Archives of General Psychiatry*, 36, 644–649.

NUECHTERLEIN, K.H. & DAWSON, M.E. (1984) A heuristic vulnerability/stress model of schizophrenic episodes. *Schizophrenia Bulletin*, 10, 300–311.

O'CALLAGHAN, E., SHAM, P.C. & TAKEI, N. (1993) Schizophrenia after prenatal exposure to 1957 A2 influenza epidemic. *The Lancet*, 337, 1248–1250.

O'CALLAGHAN, E., SHAM, P.C., TAKEI, N., MURRAY, G.K., GLOVER, G., HARE, E.H. & MURRAY, R.M. (1994) The relationship of schizophrenic births to sixteen infectious diseases. *British Journal of Psychiatry*, 165, 353–356.

O'CALLAGHAN, E., SHAM, P.C., TAKEI, N., MURRAY, G.K., HARE, E.H. & MURRAY, R.M. (1991) Schizophrenia following prenatal exposure to influenza epidemics between 1939 and 1960. *British Journal of Psychiatry*, 160, 461–466.

O'LEARY, K.D. & WILSON, G.T. (1975) *Behaviour Therapy: Application and Outcome*. Englewood Cliffs, NJ: Prentice-Hall.

OGILVIE, A.D., BATTERSBY, S., BUBB, V.J., FINK, G., HARMAR, A.J., GOODWIN, G.M. & SMITH, C.A.D. (1996) Polymorphism in the serotonin transporter gene associated with susceptibility to major depression. *The Lancet*, 347, 731–733.

OSMOND, H. & SMYTHIES, J. (1953) Schizophrenia: A new approach. *The Journal of Mental Science*, 98, 309–315.

PAPP, L.A., KLEIN, D.F., MARTINEZ, J., SCHNEIER, F., COLE, R., LIEBOWITZ, M.R., HOLLANDER, E., FYER, A.J., JORDAN, F. & GORMAN, J.M. (1993) Diagnostic and substance specificity of recent life-stress experience. *Journal of Consulting and Clinical Psychology*, 51, 467–469.

PARK, R.J., LAWRIE, J.M. & FREEMAN, C.P. (1995) Post-viral onset of anorexia nervosa. *British Journal of Psychology*. 166, 386–389.

PARKIN, J.R. & EAGLES, J.M. (1993) Blood-letting in anorexia nervosa. *British Journal of Psychiatry*, 162, 246–248.

PARRY-JONES, W.Ll. & PARRY-JONES, B. (1993) Self-mutilation in four historical cases of bulimia. *British Journal of Psychiatry*, 163, 394–402.

PATON, D. (1992) Disaster research: The Scottish dimension. *The Psychologist*, 5, 535–538.

PERLBERG, M. (1979) Trauma at Tenerife: The psychic aftershocks of a jet disaster. *Human Behaviour*, 49–50.

PETKOVA, B. (1997) Understanding eating disorders: A perspective from feminist psychology. *Psychology Review*, 4, 2–7.

PICKERING, J. (1981) Perception. *In Psychological Processes: Units 5 & 6–7*. Milton Keynes: The Open University Press.

PIRAN, N., KENNEDY, S., GARFINKEL, P.E. & OWENS, M. (1985) Affective disturbance in eating disorders. *Journal of Nervous and Mental Disease*, 173, 395–400.

POLIVY, J. & HERMAN, C.P. (1985) Dieting and bingeing: Causal analysis. *American Psychologist*, 40, 193–201.

POST, F. (1994) Creativity and psychopathology. A study of 291 world-famous men. *British Journal of Psychiatry*, 165, 22–34.

PYNOOS, R.S., GOENIJIAN, A., TASHJIAN, M., KARAKASHIAN, M., MANJIKAN, R., MANOUKIAN, G., STEINBERG, A.M. & FAIRBANKS, L.A. (1993) Post–traumatic stress reactions in children after the 1988 Armenian earthquake. *British Journal of Psychiatry*, 163, 239–247.

RACHMAN, S. (1977) *Fear and Courage*. San Francisco: W.H. Freeman.

RACHMAN, S. (1984) Agoraphobia – a safety signal perspective. *Behaviour Research and Therapy*, 22, 59–70.

ROSE, S., LEWONTIN, R.C., & KAMIN, L.J. (1984) *Not in our Genes: Biology, Ideology and Human Nature*. Harmondsworth: Penguin.

ROSENHAN, D.L. & SELIGMAN, M.E. (1984) *Abnormal Psychology*. New York: Norton.

ROSENTHAL, D. (Ed.) (1963) *The Genain Quadruplets*. New York: Basic Books.

ROY, A. (1981) Role of past loss in depression. *Archives of General Psychiatry*, 38, 301–302.

RUDERMAN, A.J. (1986) Dietary restraint: A theoretical and empirical review. *Psychological Bulletin*, 99, 247–262.

RUDOLPH, K., WIRZ-JUSTICE, A. & KRAUCHI, K. (1993) Static magnetic fields decrease nocturnal pineal cAMP in the rat. *Brain Research*, 446, 159–160.

RUSSELL, G.F.M. (1979) Bulimia nervosa: An ominous variant of anorexia nervosa. *Psychological Medicine*, 9, 429–448.

SAHAKIAN, B. (1987) Anorexia nervosa and bulimia nervosa. In R.L. Gregory (Ed.) *The Oxford Companion to the Mind*. Oxford: Oxford University Press.

SANAVIO, E. (1988) Obsessions and compulsions: The Padua Inventory. *Behaviour Research and Therapy*, 26, 169–177.

SANE (1993) Depression and Manic Depression: *The Swings and Roundabouts of the Mind*. London: SANE Publications.

SARBIN, T.R. (1992) The social construction of schizophrenia. In W. Flack, D.R. Miller & M. Wiener (Eds) *What is Schizophrenia*? New York: Springer-Verlag.

SCHILDKRAUT, J. (1965) The catecholamine hypothesis of affective disorders: A review of supporting evidence. *American Journal of Psychiatry*, 122, 509–522.

SCHNEIDER, K. (1959) *Clinical Psychopathology*. New York: Grune & Stratton.

SCOTT, J. (1994) Cognitive therapy. *British Journal of Psychiatry*, 164, 126–130.

SELIGMAN, M.E.P. (1973) Fall into hopelessness. *Psychology Today*, 7, 43–47.

SELIGMAN, M.E.P. & MAIER, S.F. (1967) Failure to escape traumatic shock. *Journal of Experimental Psychology*, 74, 1–9.

SHARP, C.W. & FREEMAN, C.P.L. (1993) The medical complications of anorexia nervosa. *British Journal of Psychiatry*, 162, 452–462.

SIMMONDS, M. (1914) Über Hypophysisschwund mit todlichem Ausung. *Deutsche Medizinische Wochenschrift*, 40, 332–340.

SKINNER, B.F. (1948) Superstition in the pigeon. *Journal of Experimental Psychology*, 38, 168–172.

SLATER, E. & ROTH, M. (1969) *Clinical Psychiatry* (3rd edition). Ballière-Tindall and Cassell.

SLATER, E. & SHIELDS, J. (1969) Genetic aspects of anxiety. In M. Lader (Ed.) *Studies of Anxiety*. Ashford, England: Headley Brothers.

SMITH, K.A., FAIRBURN, C.G. & COWEN, P.J. (1997) Relapse of depression after rapid depletion of tryptophan. *The Lancet*, 349, 915–919.

SMYTHIES, J. (1976) Recent progress in schizophrenia research. *The Lancet*, 2, 136–139.

SPITZER, R.L., SKODAL, A.E., GIBBON, M. & WILLIAMS, J.B.W. (Eds) (1981) *DSM-III Case Book*. Washington, DC: American Psychiatric Association.

STEVENS, J.R. (1982) Neurology and neuropathology of schizophenia. In F.A. Henn & G.A. Nasrallah (Eds) *Schizophrenia as a Brain Disease*. New York: Oxford University Press.

STROBER, M. & KATZ, J.L. (1987) Do eating disorders and affective disorders share a common aetiology? *International Journal of Eating Disorders*, 6, 171–180.

SUE, D., SUE, D. & SUE, S. (1994) *Understanding Abnormal Behaviour* (4th edition). Boston: Houghton-Mifflin.

SUI–WAH, L. (1989) Anorexia nervosa and Chinese food. *British Journal of Psychiatry*, 155, 568.

SULSER, F. (1979) Pharmacology: New cellular mechanisms of anti-depressant drugs. In S. Fielding & R.C. Effland (Eds) *New Frontiers in Psychotropic Drug Research*. Mount Kisco, NY: Futura.

SUNDAY, S.R. & HALMI, K.A. (1990) Taste perceptions and hedonics in eating disorders. *Physiology and Behaviour*, 48, 587–594.

SYAL, R. (1997) Doctors find pick-me-up for SAD people. *The Sunday Times*, 19 January, 4.

TALLIS, F. (1994) Obsessive-compulsive disorder. *The Psychologist*, 7, 312.

TALLIS, F. (1995) *Obsessive Compulsive Disorder: A Cognitive and Neuropsychological Perspective*. Chichester: Wiley.

TEASDALE, J. (1988) Cognitive vulnerability to persistent depression. *Cognition and Emotion*, 2, 247–274.

TEUTING, P., ROSEN, S. & HIRSCHFELD, R. (1981) *Special Report on Depression Research*. Washington, DC: NIMH-DHHS Publication No. 81–1085.

THOMPSON, S.B.N. (1997) War experiences and post-traumatic stress disorder. *The Psychologist*, 10, 349–350.

TORREY, E.F. (1988) *Surviving Schizophrenia* (revised edition). New York: Harper & Row.

TORREY, E.F., TORREY, B.B. & PETERSON, M.R. (1977) Seasonality of schizophrenic births in the United States. *Archives of General Psychiatry*, 34, 1065–1070.

TOUYZ, S.W., O'SULLIVAN, B.T., GERTLER, R. & BEAUMONT, P.J.V. (1988) Anorexia nervosa in a woman blind since birth. *British Journal of Psychiatry*, 153, 248–249.

TREASURE, J.L. & HOLLAND, A.J. (1991) Genes and the aetiology of eating disorders. In P. McGuffin & R. Murray (Eds) *The New Genetics of Mental Illness*. Oxford: Butterworth.

UHLIG. R. (1996) Superwaif Sindy 'is shaping future of girls aged eight'. *The Daily Telegraph*, 14 September, 9.

ULLMAN, L.P. & KRASNER, L. (1969) *A Psychological Approach to Abnormal Behaviour.* Englewood Cliffs, NJ: Prentice-Hall.

VAN DER KOLK, B.A., PITMAN, R.K. & ORR, S.P. (1989) Endogenous opioids, stress-induced analgesia and post-traumatic stress disorder. *Psychopharmacology Bulletin*, 25, 108–112.

WALLER, G. (1993) Sexual abuse and eating disorders. *British Journal of Psychiatry*, 162, 771–775.

WATSON, J.B. & RAYNER, R. (1920) Conditioned emotional responses. *Journal of Experimental Psychology*, 3, 1–14.

WEAVER, M. (1996) We are watching your weight, skinny Vogue models warned. *The Daily Telegraph*, 31 May, 3.

WEHR, T. & ROSENTHAL, N. (1989) Seasonability and affective illness. *American Journal of Psychiatry*, 146, 201–204.

WEISSMAN, M. (1987) Advances in psychiatric epidemiology: Rates and risks for major depression. *American Journal of Public Health*, 77, 445–451.

WEISSMAN, M. & PAYKEL, E. (1974) *The Depressed Woman.* Chicago: University of Chicago Press.

WENDER, P.H., KETY, S.S., ROSENTHAL, D., SCHULSINGER, F., ORTMANN, J. & LUNDE, I. (1986) Psychiatric disorders in the biological and adoptive families of individuals with affective disorders. *Archives of General Psychiatry*, 43, 923–929.

WENDER, P.H. & KLEIN, D.F. (1981) The promise of biological psychiatry. *Psychology Today*, 15, 25–41.

WESTHEAD, R. (1996) Power line link to the baby blues. *The Sunday Telegraph*, 15 September, 2.

WHITE, J., DAVISON, G.C. & WHITE, M. (1985) 'Cognitive distortions in the articulated thoughts of depressed patients.' (Unpublished manuscript, University of Southern California, Los Angeles.)

WHITTELL, G. (1995) Spectacular northern lights linked to suicidal depression. *The Times*, 15 April, 9.

WILLIAMS, J.M.G. & HARGREAVES, I.R. (1995) Neuroses: Depressive and anxiety disorders. In A.A. Lazarus & A.M. Colman (Eds) *Abnormal Psychology*. London: Longman.

WOLPE, J. (1969) For phobia: A hair of the hound. *Psychology Today*, 3, 34–37.

WOOLEY, S. & WOOLEY, O. (1983) Should obesity be treated at all? *Psychiatric Annals*, 13, 884–885.

WURTMAN, R. & WURTMAN, J. (1989) Carbohydrates and depression. *Scientific American*, 251, 68–75.

WYNNE, L.C., SINGER, M.T., BARTKO, J.J. & TOOHEY, M.L. (1977) Schizophrenics and their families: Recent research on parental communication. In J.M. Tanner (Ed.) *Developments in Psychiatric Research*. London: Hodder & Stoughton.

YAGER, J., HATTON, C.A. & LAWRENCE, M. (1986) Anorexia nervosa in a woman totally blind since the age of two. *British Journal of Psychiatry*, 149, 506–509.

YULE, W. (1993) Children's trauma from transport disasters. *The Psychologist*, 7, 318–319.

# INDEX